THE
REFERENCE
SHELF

WITHDRAWN

CRIME IN AMERICA

Edited by SUZANNE ELIZABETH KENDER

THE REFERENCE SHELF

Volume 68 Number 5

THE H. W. WILSON COMPANY

New York   Dublin   1996

THE REFERENCE SHELF

The books in this series contain reprints of articles, excerpts from books, and addresses on current issues and social trends in the United States and other countries. There are six numbers to a volume, all of which are usually published in a single calendar year. Numbers one through five devote themselves to a single subject, give background information and discussion from various points of view, concluding with a comprehensive bibliography that contains books, pamphlets, and abstracts of additional articles on the subject. The final number is a collection of recent speeches. This number also contains a subject index to the entire Reference Shelf volume. Books in the series may be purchased individually or on subscription.

Visit our web site at: http://www.hwwilson.com

Library of Congress Cataloging-in-Publication Data

Main entry under title:

Crime in America / edited by Suzanne Elizabeth Kender.
    p.   cm. — (The reference shelf ; v. 68, no. 5)
  Includes bibliographical references.
  ISBN 0-8242-0890-0
  1. Crime—United States.   2. Violence—United States.   3. Violent crimes—United States.   I. Kender, Suzanne Elizabeth. II. Series.
  HV6789.C6815   1996
  364.973—dc20
                                                        96-41345
                                                            CIP

Cover: A criminal is ushered into a police station. *Photo*: Bettmann

Printed in the United States of America

CONTENTS

PREFACE

What is the truth about crime in America? Statistics say that the crime rate is down in cities across the country. In 1994 there was a decrease of 8 percent in crimes of violence in nine cities with a population of one million or more, and the overall murder rate for the United States dropped 12 percent in the early part of 1995. The rate of other crimes, reports say, dropped from 1 to 2 percent. The suburbs too showed declines in violent crime. Experts attribute these drops to a variety of factors, ranging from a leveling off in the use of crack cocaine (which had fueled a crime wave in the late 1980s) to a modest rise in the employment rate, but the one factor most often mentioned is a decline in the actual number of young males in the general population. There are now fewer people in the "crime-prone" category, which is defined as males between the ages of 15 and 29 years, than there have been since the 1960s, when the "baby boomers" came of age.

These statistics sound comforting, but they hardly account for such things as the number of homicides committed in Minneapolis in 1995—56 percent more than in 1994. Nor do they take into consideration the fact that many of the teenagers now entering the "crime-prone" demographic already have criminal histories—as a group, they seem *more* prone to violence than yesterday's teenagers. And there is little comfort in knowing that most of the crimes they commit, at least most of the *violent* crimes, will be against each other.

The articles collected in this volume attempt to answer the questions of just what crime is in America, who is committing these crimes, and what we can expect in the future. The articles are broken down into three sections. Section one provides an overview of crime in America, presenting statistics and demographic information (sometimes contradictory), as reported by experts, sociologists, and criminologists.

Section two explores the root causes of crime in America. These include all the things we most expect to hear about: poverty, unemployment, drug and alcohol addiction, and the breakdown of society's traditional support systems—the family, the neighborhood community, and the educational system. But there are other, less readily understood, possible causes, involving biological rather than environmental factors. Here again, authors disagree on the validity and significance of the data, and the extent to which any one factor can be singled out as *the* cause of criminal behavior.

The third section looks at some of the long-term solutions proposed for the problem of crime, as well as some short-term preventative measures that have actually been tried. These include "more effective policing" (a phrase discussed and defined in many of the articles), improving the educational system, and improving the criminal justice system, particularly the prisons. At the individual level, one article suggests suing the government for not protecting its citizens, while another advocates bearing arms to ensure one's safety. Whatever the outcome of America's "war on crime," there are sure to be more casualties. But perhaps with enough information and education, this number can be kept to a minimum.

In closing, the editor would like to thank the authors of the articles included in this volume for helping to shed light on this topic, as well as the journals and publications which granted permission to reprint the information.

Suzanne Elizabeth Kender

September 1996

I. AN OVERVIEW

EDITOR'S INTRODUCTION

Adam Walinsky, writing for the *Atlantic Monthly*, tells us that the Department of Justice has estimated that 83 percent of all Americans will be victims of a violent crime at least once in their lives, and that 25 percent would be victims of three or more such crimes. But though reported evidence seems to support these numbers, not all are convinced of widespread danger. Patrick McCormick in his *U.S. Catholic* article, "Crime in America: Just the Facts, Ma'am," explains that though there is a heightened fear of crime among middle- and upper-class Americans, studies show that these people are the least likely to be victimized by violent crime and are, in fact, safer than they were twenty years ago. McCormick goes on to explain that crime in America tends to be concentrated in poor, inner-city neighborhoods, and preys on victims who are young, black, and male; and that currently in the United States, 16–19 year olds are more likely than the elderly to be victims of crime. But not everybody outside this high-risk category feels assured of safety. An article in *Modern Maturity* indicates that older people are just as likely as the young to be on the receiving end of crime—especially robbery—and quotes several first-hand accounts. Then there was Davis Shotkoski, a young baseball player who had come to West Palm Beach for spring training. He was shot to death when he refused to hand over his money to a gunman. In "Crime in America: It's Going to Get Worse," John DiIulio, Jr., predicts that we will hear more stories like his. DiIulio warns us that not only is the crime problem in the U.S. getting worse, it is getting more violent. "Redrawing the Face of Crime," reprinted from *Society*, offers more insight into the question of just who is committing crimes. We are told that the reality of crime differs greatly from its image: six out of ten prisoners are educated, nearly half are white or Hispanic, and less than half were raised in single-parent families.

Regardless of the conflicting views and statistics facing us in our exploration of crime in America, there is one thing that cannot be denied: crime and violence exist, and exist in our schools. A special report from *KAPPAN* paints a chilling picture of this aspect of the problem.

THE CRISIS OF PUBLIC ORDER[1]

Numbers are useful in politics, because they are more neutral than adjectival speech and because they express magnitude—that is, they can tell us not only that we confront a danger but also what the depth and direction of the danger are. The most important numbers in America deal with violence—not the occasional terrorist violence but the terror of everyday life as it is lived by millions of citizens today, and as it threatens to become for many more of us for the rest of this century and beyond.

During his campaign and since, President Bill Clinton has spoken of a sharp decline in the strength of the nation's police forces. In the 1960s the United States as a whole had 3.3 police officers for every violent crime reported per year. In 1993 it had 3.47 violent crimes reported for every police officer. In relation to the amount of violent crime, then, we have less than one tenth the effective police power of thirty years ago; or, in another formulation, each police officer today must deal with 11.45 times as many violent crimes as his predecessor of years gone by.

Title I of the 1994 crime bill intends to add 100,000 police officers nationally by the year 2000. (Most experts believe that far fewer new officers—perhaps 25,000—will actually be hired. For the purposes of this argument, though, let us assume the larger figure.) There are now some 554,000 officers serving on all state and local police forces; 100,000 more would be an increase of 18.4 percent. Rather than having 3.47 times as many violent crimes as police officers, we would have 2.94 times as many; or, each police officer would face not 11.45 times as many violent crimes as his predecessor but 9.7 times as many. All this assumes that the number of violent crimes will not increase over the next

[1]Article by Adam Walinsky from *The Atlantic Monthly* 276/1:39–54. Copyright © 1995 by Adam Walinsky as first published in the July 1995 issue of *The Atlantic Monthly*. Reprinted with permission.

several years; if it does, the number of violent crimes relative to police officers will again increase.

If we wished to return to the ratio of police officers to violent crimes which gave many of us peace and security in the 1960s, we would have to add not 100,000 new police officers but about *five million*. When this number was mentioned to some Department of Justice staffers recently, they giggled; and it is understandable that the idea of such a national mobilization, such tremendous expenditures, should strike them as laughable. However, the American people are already paying out of their own pockets for an additional 1.5 million private police officers, to provide, at least in part, the protection that the public police are unable to furnish.

Private police guard office buildings, shopping malls, apartments. Businesses pay them to patrol certain downtown streets, such as those around New York's Grand Central Station and public library. And they patrol residential areas. Private patrol cars thread the streets of Los Angeles, and more than fifty applications are before the city council to close off streets so as to make those patrols more effective. Across the country much new housing is being built in gated communities, walled off, and privately guarded. We are well on the way to having several million police officers, and the next decade will bring us much closer. If current trends continue, however, most of the new officers will be privately paid, available for the protection not of the citizenry as a whole—and certainly not of citizens living in the most violent ghettos and housing projects—but of the commercial and residential enclaves that can afford them. Between these enclaves there will be plenty of room to lose a country.

One Long Descending Night

People hire police officers because they are afraid—above all of violence. Their fear is occasionally a source of puzzlement and mild disdain in the press, which cannot understand why so many Americans say that crime is the nation's most urgent problem and their own greatest fear. Indeed, all through 1993 official agencies claimed that crime was declining. The FBI said that violent crime in the first six months was down three percent overall, and down eight percent in the Northeast.

For crime to be down even eight percent would mean that a precinct that had had a hundred murders in 1992 had ninety-two in 1993. But nobody came around on New Year's Day of 1993 to give everyone's memory a rinse, obliterating the horrors of the previous year. The effect is not disjunctive but cumulative. By the end of 1993, ninety-two additional people had been murdered.

Many people can also remember years before 1992, in large cities and in small. In 1960, for example, 6 murders, 4 rapes, and 16 robberies were reported in New Haven, Connecticut. In 1990 that city, with a population 14 percent smaller, had 31 murders, 168 rapes, and 1,784 robberies: robbery increased more than 100 times, or *10,000 percent*, over thirty years. In this perspective a one-year decrease of 7 percent would seem less than impressive.

New Haven is not unique. In Milwaukee in 1965 there were 27 murders, 33 rapes, and 214 robberies, and in 1990, when the city was smaller, there were 165 murders, 598 rapes, and 4,472 robberies: robbery became twenty-one times as frequent in twenty-five years. New York City in 1951 had 244 murders; every year for more than a decade it has had nearly 2,000 murders.

We experience the crime wave not as separate moments in time but as one long descending night. A loved one lost echoes in the heart for decades. Every working police officer knows the murder scene: the shocked family and neighbors, too numb yet to grieve; fear and desolation spreading to the street, the workplace, the school, the home, creating an invisible but indelible network of anguish and loss. We have experienced more than 20, 000 such scenes every year for more than a decade, and few of them have been truly forgotten.

The memory of a mugging may fade but does not vanish. Nine percent of those responding to a recent poll in *New York Newsday* said that they had been mugged or assaulted in the past year. This suggests an annual total for the city of more than 600, 000 muggings and assaults (remember also that many people, in poor neighborhoods especially, are assaulted more than once). That would be 4 times as many robberies and assaults as are reported to the police department. The Department of Justice says that not three quarters but only half of all violent crimes go unreported: it may be that many report as having happened "last year" an incident from more than a year ago.

Nevertheless, these are stunning numbers, especially when some other common crimes are added in. Eight percent of those polled (implying 560,000 New Yorkers) said their houses or apartments had been broken into; 22 percent (1,540,000) said their cars had been broken into. In all, 42 percent (nearly three million New Yorkers) said they had been the victims of crime in 1993. And, of course, about 2,000 were murdered. This is what it means to say that crime in 1993 was down 8 percent.

In October of 1994 the Bureau of Justice Statistics reported that violent crime had not, after all, declined in 1993 but had risen by 5.6 percent.

Several years ago the Department of Justice estimated that 83 percent of all Americans would be victims of violent crime at least once in their lives. About a quarter would be victims of three or more violent crimes. We are progressing steadily toward the fulfillment of that prediction.

A Twenty-Year Fraud Exposed

Our greatest fear is of violence from a nameless, faceless stranger. Officials have always reassured citizens by stating that the great majority of murders, at any rate, are committed by a relative or an acquaintance of the victim's; a 1993 Department of Justice report said the figure for 1988 was eight out of ten.

Unfortunately, that report described only murders in which the killer was known to prosecutors and an arrest was made. It did not mention that more and more killers remain unknown and at liberty after a full police investigation; every year the police make arrests in a smaller proportion of murder cases. In our largest cities the police now make arrests in fewer than three out of five murder cases. In other words, two out of every five killers are completely untouched by the law.

When a killing is a family tragedy, or takes place between friends or acquaintances, the police make an arrest virtually every time. When the police make an arrest, they say that the crime has been "cleared"; the percentage of crimes for which they make arrests is referred to as the clearance rate. Because murder has historically been a matter principally among families and friends, the homicide clearance rate in the past was often greater than 95 percent, even in the largest cities. As late as 1965 the national homicide clearance rate was 91 percent. However, as crime has spread and changed its character over the past generation, clearance rates have steadily dropped. In the past two years the national homicide clearance rate averaged 65.5 percent. The rate in the sixty-two largest cities is 60.5 percent. In the very largest cities—those with populations over a million—the rate is 58.3 percent.

The missing killers are almost certainly not family members, friends, or neighbors. Rather, they are overwhelmingly strangers to their victims, and their acts are called "stranger murders." Here is the true arithmetic: The 40 percent of killings in which city police departments are unable to identify and arrest perpetrators must overwhelmingly be counted as stranger murders; let us assume that 90 percent of them are committed by killers unknown to the victims. That number is equivalent to 36 percent of the total of all city murders. We know that of the 60 percent of killers the police do succeed in arresting, 20 percent have murdered strangers. That is, they have committed 12 percent of all murders. As best we can count, then, at least 48 percent of city murders are now being committed by killers who are not relatives or acquaintances of the victims.

This simple arithmetic has been available to the government and its experts for years. However, the first government document to acknowledge these facts was the FBI's annual report on crime in the United States for 1993, which was released last December. The FBI now estimates that 53 percent of all homicides are being committed by strangers. For more than two decades, as homicide clearance rates have plummeted, law-enforcement agencies have continued to assure the public that four fifths of all killings are the result of personal passions. Thus were we counseled to fear our loved ones above all, to regard the family hearth as the most dangerous place. Now that falsehood has been unmasked: the FBI tells us that actually 12 percent of all homicides take place within the family. I have heard no public official anywhere in the United States say a word about any of this.

There is another important aspect to the arithmetic: the odds facing a robber or holdup man as he decides whether to let his victim live. Again, at least 48 percent of city homicides are stranger murders, but only 12 percent of city homicides result in arrest. That is, the odds that a holdup man who kills a stranger will be arrested appear to be one in four. The Department of Justice tells us that of all those who are arrested for murder, 73 percent will be convicted of some crime; and when convicted, the killers of strangers tend to get the heaviest penalties. Nevertheless, the cumulative chances of getting clean away with the murder of a stranger are greater than 80 percent. Street thugs may be smarter than they are usually given credit for being. They do not consult government reports, but they appear to know the facts. New York bodega workers have experienced an increasing incidence of holdups ending in murder even when they have offered no resistance. Killing eliminates the possibility of witness identification.

Murder is the most frightening crime, but is the least common. Much more frequent are robbery and assault. Robbery, the forcible taking of property from the person of the victim, is the crime most likely to be committed by a stranger; 75 percent of victims are robbed by strangers. Aggravated assault, the use of a weapon or other major force with the intention of causing serious bodily harm, is the most common violent crime; 58 percent of aggravated assaults are committed by strangers.

Attacks across racial lines are a special case of crimes by strangers. Most crimes, including 80 percent of violent crimes, are committed by persons of the same race as their victims. However, the experiences of blacks and whites diverge in some respects. In cases involving a lone offender, 56 percent of white and Hispanic robbery victims report that their assailant was white or Hispanic and 40 percent that he was black. When two or more robbers commit the crime, white and Hispanic victims 38 percent of the time report them to be white or Hispanic, 46 percent of the time black, and 10 percent of the time mixed. About eight percent of black victims, in contrast, are robbed by whites or Hispanics, and more than 85 percent by blacks, whether the offenders are alone or in groups. Blacks and whites are robbed equally—75 percent of the time—by strangers, but as these figures indicate, whites are far more likely to be robbed by strangers of a different race.

This result occurs because there are many more white people and many more white victims: 87 percent of all violent crimes are committed against whites and Hispanics. In robberies lone white offenders select white victims 96 percent of the time, and lone black offenders select white victims 62 percent of the time. White rapists select white victims 97 percent of the time; black rapists select white victims 48 percent of the time. Whites committing aggravated assault attack blacks in three percent of cases; blacks commit about half their assaults against whites.

When all violent crimes are taken together, 58 percent of white victims and 54 percent of black victims report that their assailant was a stranger. Citizens of all races who are fearful of random violence have good reason for their concern. Storekeepers, utility workers, police officers, and ordinary citizens out for a carton of milk or a family dinner are all increasingly at risk.

Toward a Race Behind Bars

In 1990 federal, state, and local governments combined spent about $8,921 per person. According to the Department of Justice, these governments spent $299 per person—about 3.3 percent of total public expenditures—on all civil and criminal justice activities, including $128 per person on domestic police protection. On national defense and international relations they spent $1,383 per person.

Spending on the Armed Forces has historically risen to meet perceived threats from hostile nations, or in case of rebellion. Sharply rising crime rates have not brought equivalent increases in police forces. From 1971 to 1990, as the rates of homicide and other violent crimes soared, per person expenditures (in constant dollars) on state and local police forces increased by only 12 percent.

Spending did increase on prisons—by more than 150 percent. In 1992 state and federal prisons held 883,656 inmates (local jails held another 444,584). Out of every 100,000 residents of the United States, 344 were in prison (another 174 were in jail). Prison populations increased another seven percent in 1993, by which year 2.9 times as many people were incarcerated as had been in 1980.

The overwhelming majority of prison inmates are male. Of the 789,700 male inmates in 1992, 51 percent, or 401,700, were black, and nearly all the remaining 388,000 white. (Here Hispanics are included in both categories; according to the Department of Justice, 93 percent of Hispanic prisoners describe themselves as white and seven percent as black. Asians and Native Americans make up at most 2.5 percent of all prisoners.) Rates of imprisonment by race are therefore very different. In 1992, of every 100,000 white and Hispanic male residents, 372 were prisoners. Of every 100,000 black male residents, 2,678 were prisoners.

The heaviest rates of imprisonment affect men aged twenty to forty. Although the overall imprisonment rate for black men is 2,678 per 100,000, it reaches 7,210 for every 100,000 aged twenty-five to twenty-nine, and 6,299 for those aged thirty to thirty-four. At any one time 6 to 7 percent of black men at these critical ages are in state and federal prisons.

(Most arrests, and most new prison sentences, are not for violent crimes. In 1992 only 28.5 percent of offenders sentenced to state prisons had been convicted of violent offenses; 31.2 percent had been convicted of property offenses, and 30.5 percent of drug offenses. These numbers represent a major change in just over a decade: in 1980, 48.2 percent of newly sentenced offenders had been convicted of violent offenses, and only 6.8 percent of drug offenses. The Department of Justice has argued that many people convicted of nonviolent drug crimes have also committed violent offenses. But there can be no question that the police are making more drug arrests and relatively fewer arrests for violent crimes. For the past five years drug arrests have averaged one million a year, and arrests for all violent crimes combined about 600,000.)

A study was made of black men aged eighteen to thirty-four in the District of Columbia. On any given day in 1991, 15 percent of the men were in prison, 21 percent were on probation or parole, and six percent were being sought by the police or were on bond awaiting trial. The total thus involved with the criminal justice system was 42 percent. The study estimated that 70 percent of black men in the District of Columbia would be arrested before the age of thirty-five, and that 85 percent would be arrested at some point in their lives.

There have been no studies of the effects of such high imprisonment rates on the wider black society—for example, on the children of prisoners. No government or private agency has suggested any way to lighten the influence of paternal and sibling imprisonment on children, or how to balance the potential value of such an effort against the need to suppress violent crimes. Although the crime bill will substantially expand prison space, no one has asked how much further we can go—whether it is possible, practically, socially, or morally, to imprison some larger proportion of the black male population at any one time.

What's Already Spoken For

In 1965 Daniel Patrick Moynihan warned that a growing proportion of black children were being born to single mothers. When such large numbers of children were abandoned by their fathers and brought up by single mothers, he said, the result was sure to be wild violence and social chaos. He was excoriated as a racist and the subject was abandoned. The national rate of illegitimacy among blacks that year was 26 percent.

It took just over a decade for the black illegitimacy rate to reach 50 percent. And in 1990, twenty-five years after Moynihan's warning, two thirds of black children were born to single mothers, many of them teenagers. Only a third of black children lived with both parents even in the first three years of their lives. Seven percent of all black children and 5 percent of black children under the age of three were living with neither a father nor a mother in the house. The rate of illegitimacy more than doubled in one generation.

Social disorder—in its many varieties, and with the assistance of government policies—can perhaps be said to have caused the sudden collapse of family institutions and social bonds that had survived three centuries of slavery and oppression. It is at any rate certain that hundreds of thousands of the children so abandoned have become in their turn a major cause of instability. Most notably they have tended to commit crimes, especially violent crimes, out of all proportion to their numbers. Of all juveniles confined for violent offenses today, less than 30 percent grew up with both parents.

How many killers are there, and who are they? In 1990 a total of 24,932 homicides were reported. Of all killers identified by the nation's police forces and reported to the Department of Justice for that year, 43.7 percent were white and Hispanic and 54.7 percent were black. Whites made up 83.9 percent of the population that year, and blacks 12.3 percent. The rate of homicide committed by whites was thus 5.2 per 100,000, and by blacks 44.7 per 100,000—or about eight times as great. In the large counties analyzed by the Department of Justice, 62 percent of identified killers were black. This is equivalent to a black homicide rate of 50.7 per 100,000—close to ten times the rate among other citizens. Serial killers and mass murderers, however, are overwhelmingly white.

Of the urban killers identified by the Department of Justice in 1988, 90 percent were male. Virtually none were aged fourteen or younger, but 16 percent were aged fifteen to nineteen, 24 percent were twenty to twenty-four, and 20 percent were twenty-five to twenty-nine.

The white and black populations each suffered about 12,000 homicides in 1990. But the black population base is smaller, and the rate at which blacks fall victim is much higher. The victimization rate for white males was 9.0 per 100,000, and for white females 2.8 per 100,000. For black males it was an astonishing 69.2, and for black females it was 13.5. According to the Department of Justice, one out of every twenty-one black men can expect to be murdered. This is a death rate double that of American servicemen in the Second World War.

Prospects for the future are apparent in the facts known about children already born. This is what Senator Moynihan means when he says the next thirty years are "already spoken for."

We first notice the children of the ghetto when they grow muscles—at about the age of fifteen. The children born in 1965 reached their fifteenth year in 1980, and 1980 and 1981 set new records for criminal violence in the United States, as teenage and young adult blacks ripped at the fabric of life in the black inner city. Nevertheless, of all the black children who reached physical maturity in those years, three quarters had been born to a married mother and father. Not until 1991 did we experience the arrival in their mid-teens of the first group of black youths fully half of whom had been born to single mothers—the cohort born in 1976. Criminal violence particularly associated with young men and boys reached new peaks of destruction in black communities in 1990 and 1991.

In the year 2000 the black youths born in 1985 will turn fifteen. Three fifths of them were born to single mothers, many of whom were drug-addicted; one in fourteen will have been raised with neither parent at home; unprecedented numbers will have been subjected to beatings and other abuse; and most will have grown up amid the utter chaos pervading black city neighborhoods. It is supremely necessary to change the conditions that are producing such cohorts. But no matter what efforts we now undertake, we have already assured the creation of more very violent young men than any reasonable society can tolerate, and their numbers will grow inexorably for every one of the next twenty years.

In absolute numbers the teenage and young adult population aged fifteen to twenty-four stagnated or actually declined over the past decade. Crime has been rising because this smaller population has grown disproportionately more violent. Now it is about to get larger in size. James Fox, a dean at Northeastern University, in Boston, has shown that from 1965 to 1985 the national homicide rate tracked almost exactly the proportion of the population aged eighteen to twenty-four. Suddenly, in 1985, the two curves diverged sharply. The number of young adults as a proportion of the population declined; but the overall homicide rate went up, because among this smaller group the homicide rate increased by 65 percent in just eight years. Among those aged fourteen to seventeen, the next group of young adults, the homicide rate more than doubled. What we experienced from 1985 on was a conjunction of two terrible arrivals. One train carried the legacy of the 1970s, the children of the explosion of illegitimacy and paternal abandonment. Crack arrived on the same timetable, and unloaded at the same station.

Fox shows further that by the year 2005 the population aged fourteen to seventeen will have increased by a remarkable 23 percent. Professor John DeIulio, of Princeton University, predicts that the number of homicides may soon rise to 35,000 or 40,000 a year, with other violent offenses rising proportionally. Fox calls what we are about to witness an "epidemic" of teenage crime. He does not give a name to our present condition.

Guns

It is a commonplace that many crimes are committed with guns, particularly handguns. In 1993, 69.6 percent of all homicides were committed by gun, four fifths of these by handgun. Guns were also used in 42.4 percent of all robberies and 25.1 percent of aggravated assaults. The total of such gun felonies reported to the police was about 571,000.

As long as surveys have asked the question, about half of all American households have answered that they own at least one gun. Patterns of ownership, however, have changed. In the 1960s weapons used primarily for sport—rifles and shotguns—made up 80 percent of the approximately 80 million guns in private hands.

About 12 percent of the population reported owning one or more handguns. By 1976, with the great postwar crime wave under way, more than 21 percent of the population reported owning handguns—an increase of 75 percent. The largest increases were among nonwhites (by 99 percent), college graduates (by 147 percent), and Jews (by 679 percent, to a total of 14.8 percent reporting handgun ownership, which left them well behind Protestants but ahead of Catholics). By 1978 the estimate of total number of guns owned had increased to roughly 120 million.

In every year since, at least four million new guns have been manufactured or imported. In 1993 there were 5.1 million guns manufactured and another 2.9 million imported. Of the eight million new guns in 1993, half—3.9 million—were handguns. The current estimate is that more than 200 million guns are in private hands.

Twenty states allow any law-abiding citizen to carry a gun concealed on his or her person, and fourteen more states are actively considering such laws. In some of the states where the laws have passed, about 2 percent (Oregon and Florida) or 3 percent (Pennsylvania) of the state's population have applied for and received a permit to carry a concealed handgun at all times. There is evidence that many people own and carry handguns without permits. One 1991 survey reported that a third of all Americans own handguns, another that 7 percent carry them outside the home. A quarter of small business establishments may keep firearms for protection.

Last year *The New York Times* said that the city's bodegas had become "Islands Under Siege," in which fifty store workers were killed in a year. It reported on Omar Rosario, the manager of a grocery store whose previous owner was killed in a holdup. Rosario prepares for work by donning a bulletproof vest and sliding a nine-millimeter semi-automatic into his waistband. When a young man with one arm hidden inside his coat enters the store, "Mr. Rosario takes out his pistol and eases it halfway into the pocket of his pants, his finger on the trigger. He faces the man and lets him see the gun in his hand. He wants to make it clear that if the young man pulls a gun, he will be killed."

Professor Gary Kleck, of Florida State University, has made a close examination of citizens' use of firearms for self-defense, including in "civilian legal defensive homicides." Self-defense is not a crime, and most defensive uses of firearms, even when criminals are killed, are not routinely reported to the FBI. On the basis of local studies Kleck estimates that at least 1,500 citizens used guns to kill criminals in 1980. This is nearly three times the number of criminals killed by the police. The Department of Justice thinks these numbers may be too high. Nevertheless, it is evident that Omar Rosario is not the only citizen with his finger on the trigger.

Beyond the Numbers

For more than twenty years the children of the ghetto have witnessed violent death as an almost routine occurrence. They have seen it on their streets, in their schools, in their families, and on TV. They have lived with constant fear. Many have come to believe that they will not live to see twenty-five. These are often children whose older brothers, friends, and uncles have taught them that only the strong and the ruthless survive. Prison does not frighten them—it is a rite of passage that a majority of their peers may have experienced. Too many have learned to kill without remorse, for a drug territory or for an insult, because of a look or a bump on the sidewalk, or just to do it: why not?

These young people have been raised in the glare of ceaseless media violence and incitement to every depravity of act and spirit. Movies may feature scores of killings in two hours' time, vying to show methods ever more horrific; many are quickly imitated on the street. Television commercials teach that a young man requires a new pair of $120 sneakers each week. Major corporations make and sell records exhorting their listeners to brutalize Koreans, rob store owners, rape women, kill the police. Ashamed and guilt-ridden, elite opinion often encourages even hoodlums to carry a sense of entitlement and grievance against society and its institutions.

These lessons are being taught to millions of children as I write and you read. They have already been taught to the age groups that will reach physical maturity during the rest of this century.

The worst lesson we have taught these benighted children I have saved for last, because it is a lesson we have also taught ourselves: We will do almost anything not to have to act to defend ourselves, our country, or our character as people of decency and strength. We have fled from our cities, virtually abandoning great institutions such as the public schools. We have permitted the spread within our country of wastelands ruled not by the Constitution and lawful authority but by the anarchic force of merciless killers. We have muted our dialogue and hidden our thoughts. We have abandoned millions of our fellow citizens—people of decency and honor trying desperately to raise their children in love and hope—to every danger and degraded assault. We have become isolated from one another, dispirited about any possibility of collective or political action to meet this menace. We shrink in fear of teenage thugs on every street. More important, we shrink even from contemplating the forceful collective action we know is required. We abandon our self-respect and our responsibility to ourselves and our posterity.

How to change all this, how to recover heart and spirit, how to save the lives and souls of millions of children, and how to save ourselves from this scourge of violent anarchy—in short, how to deal with things as they are, how to respond to the implacable and undeniable numbers: this will be the real measure and test of our political system. But more than that, it will be the measure of our own days and work, the test of our own lives and heritage.

Where Do We Start? A Modest Radicalism

In the past decade 200,000 of our citizens have been killed and millions wounded. If we assume, with the FBI, that 47 percent of them were killed by friends and family members, that leaves 106,000 dead at the hands of strangers. Ten years of war in Vietnam killed 58,000 Americans. Over an equal period we have had almost the exact equivalent of two Vietnam Wars right here at home.

Whether fighting the war or fighting against the war, participants and opponents alike engaged Vietnam with fury and passion and a desperate energy. Were we to find such energy, such passion, now, how might we use it? Where would we start?

I suggest simplicity. If your territory and your citizens are under constant deadly assault, the first thing you do is *protect them*.

To do this we need forces. We need a very large number of additional police officers: at least half a million in the next five years, and perhaps more thereafter. We do not need more private police, who protect only the circumscribed property of better-off citizens who can afford to pay; we need public police, whose mission is the protection of all citizens, and who are available for work in the ghettos and housing projects where most of the dying is taking place.

If we as a society expect black citizens to construct reasonable lives, we cannot continue to abandon so many of them and their children to criminal depredation. If we expect children to respect law and the rights of others, it would seem elementary that we must respect the law and their rights enough to keep them from getting murdered.

We need a larger police force not to imprison more of our fellow citizens but to liberate them. The police need not function as the intake valve of a criminal justice system devoted to the production of more prison inmates, of whom we already have more than is healthy; their true role is to suppress violence and criminal activity, to protect public space that now serves as the playground and possession of the violent. The role of the police is to guard schools and homes, neighborhoods and commerce, and to protect life; they should represent the basic codes and agreements by which we live with one another. Today's vastly undermanned police forces, whose officers race from call to call, taking endless reports of crimes they were not around to prevent, do not control the streets. They do not exercise and cannot embody the authority for which we look to government. Rather, it is the most violent young men of the street who set the tone and filter the light in which the children of the city are growing. *That* is what we need at least half a million new officers just to begin to change.

Some will ask how we are to afford the $30 billion or so a year that this would cost. The question has a ready answer. We have a gross domestic product of more than $6 trillion, and a federal budget of more than $1.6 trillion. President Clinton has requested $261.4 billion for defense against foreign enemies who killed fewer than a hundred Americans in all of last year. It would be silly to suggest that the federal government should not or cannot spend an eighth as much—two percent of even a shrunken federal budget—to defend the nation against domestic enemies who killed more than 10,000 people who were strangers to them in 1994, and who will surely kill more in every year that lies ahead.

This is not a complete program, because this is not the time for a complete program. *We have to stop the killing.* Beyond doubt we must reform welfare, minimize illegitimacy, change the schools, strengthen employment opportunities, end racism. In the midst of this war, while the killing continues, all that is just talk. And dishonest talk besides: there can be no truth to our public discussions while whites are filled with fear of black violence, and blacks live every day with the fear and bitter knowledge that they and their children have been abandoned to the rule of criminals. If some foreign enemy had invaded New England, slaughtering its people and plundering its wealth, would we be debating agricultural subsidies and the future of Medicaid while complaining that the deficit prevented us from enlarging the Army or buying more ammunition? Would the budget really force us to abandon New Hampshire? Why is this case different?

None of This Is Necessary

Some people will say that I propose an army of occupation. But all too many black citizens already live in territories occupied by hostile bands of brigands. How can these citizens be freed except by forces devoted to their liberation?

It is true that the police, especially in the ghettos of older cities, have often been corrupt, brutal, and ineffective, although they are almost always better than most of their critics. The remedy for bad policing is for good people to join the police force and make it better: that is why the one truly promising feature of the 1994 crime bill is the creation of a prototype Police Corps, a police ROTC that will offer four-year college scholarships to the best and most committed of our young people in return for four years of police service following their graduation. Now and for many years into the future the opportunity to give the greatest service to one's fellow citizens will be as a member of a police force—the one truly indispensable agency of a free and civil government.

Others will say—not openly, because this kind of thing is never said openly—that it's hopeless, and that the best we can hope for is that the killers will kill one another and leave the rest of us alone. Indeed, a visitor from another planet might well conclude that only such a belief could explain our society's otherwise inexplicable passivity. History should save us from such vile and horrible thoughts. Despite all vicissitudes, within two generations of Emancipation black families had achieved levels of stability and nurture comparable or superior to those of many immigrant groups. The long history of black people in America has not been one of violent or cruel conduct beyond the national norm. Rather, it is a story of great heroism and dignity, of a steady upward course from slavery to just the other day.

The collapse of the black lower class is a creation not of history but of this generation. It has been a deliberate if misguided act of government to create a welfare system that began the destruction of black family life. It was the dominant culture that desanctified morality, celebrated license, and glorified fecklessness; as the columnist Joe Klein has observed, it is in moral conduct above all that the rich catch cold and the poor get pneumonia. It was stupidity and cowardice, along with a purposeful impulse toward justice, that led the entire governmental apparatus, the system of law enforcement and social control, to cede the black ghettos to self-rule and virtual anarchy in the 1960s and 1970s, and to abandon them entirely since. It is the evident policy of the entertainment industry to seek profit by exploiting the most degraded aspects of human and social character. None of this is necessary. All of it can be changed.

I have spoken of the need to change conditions among blacks, because they are experiencing the greatest suffering and the gravest danger today. But let none of us pretend that the bell tolls only for blacks; there is no salvation for one race alone, no hope for separate survival. At stake for all of us is the future of American cities, the promise of the American nation, and the survival of our Constitution and of American democracy itself.

CRIME IN AMERICA: JUST THE FACTS, MA'AM[2]

Last fall, while politicians and candidates of every stripe were falling over themselves trying to prove to concerned voters that they were tougher on crime than their wimpy opponents, I had a slightly more personal encounter with the surprise hot campaign issue of '94. Somebody tried to mug me.

[2]Article by Patrick T. McCormick from *U.S. Catholic* 60/3:46-9 Mr '95, published by Claretian Publication, Chicago, IL. Copyright © 1995 by *U.S. Catholic*. Reprinted with permission.

Fortunately, thanks mainly to my assailant's incompetence and a good deal of luck, I escaped unharmed, and he was later apprehended by the local police. Still, though the incident didn't transform me into a conservative or lead to a National Rifle Association membership, I have felt its lingering impact. More than once in the last few months I've jumped at the unexpected sound of running footsteps, or glanced repeatedly over my shoulder on the nightly walk home.

Even more, however, I found myself paying closer attention to the public conversations politicians and their constituents were having about crime in America. Unfortunately I found many of these blistering exchanges—whether attacking opponents for putting too much "fat" in the crime bill, or blasting candidates for being "soft" on crime—just as disturbing as the attempted assault.

All too often politicians and pundits were content to address crime with sound-bite analysis and simplistic solutions, instead of attempting to grasp its real shape and causes or offer solutions that might be both effective and moral. Of course in the heat of a political campaign it may be unreasonable to expect candidates to challenge popular assumptions about this issue or to offer thoughtful analysis and solutions. Still, now that things have calmed down a bit, it might be helpful if we, as citizens and Christians, sat down and critically examined some of our culture's popular beliefs about crime and punishment in America, and see if we really agree with them.

To anyone in 1994 who was following the various polls, talk-show pundits, and migratory patterns of politicians, it seemed clear both that crime had replaced the economy and health care as a hot-button campaign issue and that American popular culture had some fixed beliefs about this issue. First, survey after survey indicated that a growing majority of middle- and upper-class Americans felt concerned about or threatened by crime and perceived themselves to be in the midst of an explosive and increasingly violent crime wave.

Second, popular culture clearly views this crime wave as resulting from both (a) a loss of moral and family values, and (b) the failure of our criminal-justice system (particularly the courts and politicians) to take a "tough stand" on crime. According to popular opinion, criminals—particularly dangerous ones—are coddled by a system that either excuses their outrageous conduct

because of some imagined victimization or shortens their prison
sentences to a laughable slap on the wrist.

Third, given the source and tone of the alarm being sounded,
one would assume that crime in America consisted mainly of an
assault on middle- and upper-class Americans by violent strangers
and that this recent crime wave was lapping primarily at the
shores of suburbia.

Finally, as is evident from last fall's campaign and the fuss
over the crime bill, the most popular answer to the present crisis
is to declare a "war on crime" and shift money away from prevention and social programs while investing even more resources in
prisons and police. Thus, politicians and voters clamor for stiffer
sentences, more cops, and an increasing reliance upon the death
penalty.

But although these beliefs seem well entrenched in our corporate psyche, the question remains as to whether all, or even any,
of them are true. And indeed it would seem that they are not, for
when we contrast popular perceptions about crime with some of
the statistical information, a significant gap surfaces between the
two.

To start with, in spite of the fact that there is an alarmingly
high level of criminal violence in our inner cities and among our
urban poor, a number of studies raise serious questions about
popular conceptions regarding an increasing crime rate. For example, although the majority of Americans surveyed believe that
both the overall and violent crime rates have increased dramatically since the early '70s, studies cited in last October's *Economist*
show that the overall rate of crime in America has dropped over
the past two decades. And even when the increase in violent
crimes is adjusted for population growth, there is a per capita decrease in this rate as well.

Indeed, just as last year's polls were pointing to a heightened
fear of crime in middle-class Americans, FBI reports were indi-
cating a drop in national crime rates. So whatever is spurring this
recent concern, it doesn't seem to be a sudden outbreak in the
rate of crime in our streets.

Nor does it seem to be true that America coddles its criminals.
In spite of the media hype given to high profile "abuse excuse"
homicide cases, an article in the conservative journal *Reason* notes
that courts are not normally persuaded by such insanity pleas and
such defendants are not often acquitted. Also, with more than

one million Americans currently behind bars and better than three times that number on parole or probation, our country has the dubious honor of having the highest per capita imprisonment rate in the industrial world and is one of the only modern nations that still relies on capital punishment—hardly the record of a coddler.

And though politicians and citizens love to complain about violent offenders (like Willie Horton) released after having served only a fraction of their sentences, an article in last June's *Atlantic Monthly* notes that "from 1975 to 1989 the average prison time served per violent crime tripled . . . and the prison population nearly tripled." Indeed, one of the key reasons why some violent offenders don't serve their full sentence is *not* the softness of our criminal-justice system but the fact that the 1980s' war on drugs and the accompanying strict mandatory-sentencing practices have glutted our prison system with drug offenders.

And what about all those middle- and upper-class Americans whose heightened concern about crime has gotten the attention of pollster and politician alike? Curiously enough, studies reported in both the *Economist* (October 15, 1994) and the *Wall Street Journal* (August 12, 1992) show not only that this is the population least threatened by violent crime but also that this group is actually safer today than it was two decades ago.

Indeed, numerous studies indicate that while stories of suburban wives carjacked by strangers capture the headlines and provoke moral and political outcries, the daily epidemic of violent crime in the U.S. actually tends to be concentrated in poor, inner-city neighborhoods and prefers victims that are young, poor, black, and male.

So while juveniles and blacks may commit a disproportionately large majority of violent crimes, they also constitute the largest group of its victims. In America, 16- to 19-year-olds are 20 times more likely than the elderly to be victims of violent crime, while homicide (taking the life of every 28th black male) is currently the leading cause of death among young black men. If crime has a war zone, it is not in the suburbs.

As to our "war on crime," although getting "tough" with criminals by building more prisons and imposing stiffer penalties appeals to voters, these approaches haven't reduced crime or made our streets safer. Since the early '80s we have nearly tripled our prison capacity and increased the Federal Bureau of Prison's budget over 470 percent, spending $21 to $24 billion a year on prison maintenance and construction. In the same period we have more than tripled our prison population by introducing increasingly stiffer penalties in the form of minimum mandatory sentences and different forms of Clinton's famous "three strikes" rule. And yet neither of these responses has had an appreciable effect on the rate of violent crime. Indeed, if anything, many studies indicated that instead of deterring future crimes, our increasingly massive prison system serves as a breeding ground for violent felons.

All too often our inner-city youths experience imprisonment as both a rite of passage into manhood and a training school for more serious crimes. Thus, in neighborhoods where few youths could hope to go to community colleges or get decent jobs, our society ends up footing the bill for many of these young people to get a prison "education" with a tuition of $25,000 to $75,000 a year. Perhaps, then, it's not so surprising that some of the states with the highest rates in incarceration also have the worst statistics for violent crime. If stiffer sentences and more prisons are winning the "war on crime," it is certainly a Pyrrhic victory.

At the same time, while expanding our reliance on the death penalty or beefing up our police forces are popular political responses to crime, they are not effective ones. After decades of research, supporters of the death penalty have failed to produce any evidence that this punishment serves as a deterrent to violent crime or that its use makes our streets safer—in fact, recent data makes it clear that this approach is much more expensive to taxpayers than life in prison. Also, more than one expert has suggested that capital punishment is counterproductive because it helps to desensitize citizens to violence. This could be another reason why so many civilized nations have abandoned its use and why numerous human-rights groups attack its continued employment in our country.

Further, while increasing police presence in some communities might be helpful, there are no studies justifying the call for a national buildup of our police force. Indeed, one landmark St. Louis study done in the '70s indicated that there was no correlation between a community's crime rate and the number of police assigned to it, while other research showed that although tripling the police presence in an area did increase the number of arrests, convictions, and imprisonments, it had little or no impact on the crime rate.

None of this is to say that police and prisons don't serve a valuable purpose. But these studies do indicate that a continuing shift away from the so-called soft approaches stressing education, employment, drug rehabilitation, and other forms of prevention is fatally flawed. While politicians were screaming at each other last fall for cramming too much fat in the crime bill, the National Recreation and Park Association released a nationwide study proving that recreation and training programs could and did reduce the juvenile crime rate. Likewise, prevention programs involving outreach, education, and recreation cut the juvenile crime rates in Cincinnati, Dallas, and Fort Meyers between 24 and 27 percent.

Further, though an improving economy and decreasing unemployment figures gave middle- and upper-class voters the luxury to focus on crime and cry for tough penalties, things were different in America's poorest neighborhoods. There, even though people are much more likely to encounter violent crime, the hot issues—and the solutions to crime—continue to be the economy, unemployment, drugs, and education.

Perhaps that's because they know from experience that the crime that stalks their streets is not born simply of a malice we can contain with our police or break in our prisons but flows from a despair rooted in ignorance, poverty, addiction, and unemployment.

Study after study illustrates that crime in America is concentrated in the same neighborhoods having the worst schools, most devastating poverty, highest rates of unemployment, and worst problems of addiction. Unless we address these other issues, we can build prisons and hire police till we are blue in the face, but things won't get better.

Let me bring these reflections to a close by offering three thoughts for your consideration. First, it seems to me that any amount of crime, particularly violent crime, is too much, and that police and prisons are an important part of our response to this serious problem.

On the night my assailant attacked me, I was quite upset and frightened, and when three police cars responded to my 911 call and arrested my would-be mugger, I was genuinely relieved. Still—and this is my second point—I am convinced that our society's increasing and excessive reliance on punishment, as well as the public disdain we seem to have for prevention, is not just counterproductive but may say something unflattering about us as a community.

In the *Atlantic Monthly* article mentioned previously, author Wendy Kaminer suggests that the preference for punishment over prevention may reflect a darkly moralistic view of the world, devoid of hope either in prevention or rehabilitation. That view is very problematic for Christians. One who holds such a view lacks a basic compassion for those tempted to crime and wanders very near despair in failing to hope in people's capacity for repentance or conversion.

It's hard for me to see how such a view is compatible with our belief in a God who died to save us from our sins. Or perhaps— my final point—the preference for punishment is simply a form of apathy or sloth.

If we were to admit that crime was also a social problem, or that violent crime was an epidemic with multiple socioeconomic causes, then addressing it would demand complex, long-term, and costly solutions. Dealing with crime would involve caring about what happens to those in our worst neighborhoods and making a commitment to prevention, education, employment, and rehabilitation. That would take a lot of care and work.

In the end, I think we are confronted with two basic options in responding to crime. We may continue with "politics as usual" and, as Claude Raines suggests in *Casablanca*, "round up the usual suspects." Or we might follow the advice of Pope Paul VI, who suggested that "if you want peace, work for justice."

Let's remember those options the next time a politician promises to "get tough" on crime.

BEHIND THE NUMBERS[3]

Contrary to popular belief, the overall crime rate has actually declined in recent years. At the same time, however, *fear* of crime has risen dramatically, topping the list of older Americans' concerns in a recent AARP survey. The simple explanation is that the incidence of violent crime, which according to the FBI has jumped more than 50 percent over the past decade, grabs headlines and adds drama to the nightly news.

Americans have always had a fascination with crime, simultaneously finding criminals both offensive and appealing—at least in the abstract. When police trapped Jimmy Cagney high atop a fuel tank in the movie *White Heat* and he shouted, "Made it, Ma! Top of the world!" as the tank exploded, he was at once mesmerizing and tragic. Of course, Cagney's real-life counterparts likely were not perceived as a threat to the well-being of ordinary folks. As crime has become more violent and more random, there has been a concurrent rise in popularity of the tough antihero—whether a law officer like Dirty Harry or a private citizen—who does an end run around the criminal-justice system to administer swift, sure justice of his own.

In our January–February issue we featured an article about a New Mexico man who turned the tables on a 16-year-old thug who attacked him with a club. To the youth's astonishment, the older man pulled out a pistol and shot him. The story examined the incident from all sides—victim, perpetrator, and members of the criminal-justice system—to illustrate that there are no simple answers to the problem of crime in America.

On the back cover of that same issue, we invited readers to share their own experiences with crime. Hundreds of you responded, and as we pored through accounts ranging from arguments with the neighbors to a letter from the wife of a police officer killed in the line of duty, a common thread began to emerge: To varying degrees, their encounters with crime had changed all the victims.

[3]Article by Al Cole from *Modern Maturity* 38/3:93-4 My/Ju '95. Copyright © 1995 by American Association of Retired Persons. Reprinted with permission.

No Insignificant Crimes

Research indicates that older people have been as likely as younger people to be the victims of such crimes as pocket-picking and purse-snatching. Here is one of the stories behind the statistics. "I had been Christmas shopping and had 30 minutes or so to spare before heading to my granddaughter's Christmas concert," writes a Massachusetts woman. "So I stopped at the supermarket to do a little grocery shopping. I paid for my groceries with my bank ATM card and got an extra $50 cash. I was full of Christmas spirit that day as I pushed the grocery cart toward my car. The screeching of tires interrupted the quiet of the morning, and as I turned to see where the noise was coming from, a car sped by within inches of me."

The driver suddenly reached out the window, pushed the shopping cart away, grabbed the woman's pocketbook, and was gone before she realized what was happening. "Perhaps handbag-snatching is very low on the list of violent crimes, but it was a crime of immense proportion to me. I felt devastated, angry, violated. I became obsessed with knowing where my things were. I have become paranoid and suspicious of everyone whenever I am out. How do I replace pictures of loved ones no longer with me? A special pen I've had since I graduated from nursing school long ago? A key chain made specially for me by a grandchild? An insignificant crime, maybe, as crimes go. But I am a different person now."

Taking Matters in Hand

Older robbery victims have also been more likely than younger victims to face offenders armed with guns. A South Carolina pharmacist recounts the day a few years ago when a stranger with a gun appeared behind his pharmacy counter and demanded Demerol and morphine. "My life was in the hands of a nervous, drug-crazed crook with an even more nervous trigger finger. I knew this scuzzball would shoot me for any reason—or worse, for no reason. It ended as abruptly as it started. The criminal took what he wanted and fled. But for me the memories and nightmares were just beginning. I knew that this crook was still free and for months I did not sleep well. He could have easily discovered where I live. What would he do to me or my family if he thought I could identify him and testify against him? Even now, several years later, I am still easily startled, especially when someone approaches my blind side."

The encounter spurred the reader to take responsibility for his own protection. "Since my experience, I have given much thought to how this crime might have been prevented. If the law permitted me to have a concealed weapon, this criminal would never have had the nerve to risk a robbery. The evidence in favor of a reasonable permit system is so overwhelming that I am now working to change the law in my own state."

A Dream Shattered

More than two-thirds of the violent crimes committed against older people are perpetrated by strangers. An Arizona man tells a harrowing tale of being kidnapped along with his wife by two rifle-carrying drifters near an isolated campsite. "We were driving a large moving van almost filled with building materials because we were in the process of building a home. I got out of the cab and went to the back of the van and raised the overhead door." Two gunmen approached and ordered the man to get into the back of the van with his wife. The drifters then got into the cab and sped away with the couple locked inside. The husband managed to unbolt the back door and the couple decided to jump when the van turned onto a gravel road. The man suffered only a few bruises and scratches, but his wife fractured her skull and pelvis. Police captured the gunmen five hours later.

"Life has never been the same for her since the incident," he writes. "She cannot remember anything that happened two weeks before the abduction. Her attitude toward life has turned negative. She underwent therapy for almost six years, along with taking various medications for depression. My wife and I have divorced, and she is living with her daughter in Kansas. The house was finished; I am living in it alone."

Strength in Community

There is one crime statistic that, on the surface, is good news: People 65 and over are the least likely victims of violent crimes, according to 1992 Bureau of Justice Statistics. What the numbers *don't* reveal is to what degree fear of crime is making older Americans withdraw from society.

Law-enforcement officials urge just the opposite. They recommend that older citizens get involved in community crime-prevention programs and learn more about how the criminal-justice system works, how to report suspicious activities, and how to reduce the risk of becoming crime victims themselves.

Unfortunately, writes the Brookings Institution's John DiIulio in *The Wall Street Journal*, there is little the federal government can do about the problem of crime other than encourage states to act on a couple of fronts. DiIulio, director of the Institution's Center for Public Management, argues that "crime is a subnational problem with two solutions strongly favored by wide public majorities: (1) Incarcerate violent and repeat criminals for all or most of their terms, and (2) put more police on the streets in high-crime neighborhoods."

The Quality of Mercy

It's hard to find any bright spots in these accounts—save that the victims are still around to tell the tale. But the sentiments expressed in a North Carolina man's letter stand in sharp contrast to the understandable bitterness in many of the others.

Five years ago an unseen assailant struck the then-76-year-old custodian from behind with a metal object. The man lost hearing in one ear and was partially paralyzed for 17 weeks. "The doctor who operated on my inner ear said not many younger people would have survived what I did," he writes. He still has an equilibrium problem and walks with a cane.

The man credits his recovery to prayer, his family, and his church family. "If you are a victim of crime, it is very important that you know you are loved by family and friends." He then turns the other cheek: "I have no idea who hit me. I don't know if he was young or old, or what race he is. But I have to forgive him to rightly survive myself."

CRIME IN AMERICA: IT'S GOING TO GET WORSE[4]

David Shotkoski had always dreamed of becoming a Major League pitcher. Early this year, he kissed his wife and young daughter good-bye and left North Aurora, Ill., for spring training with the Atlanta Braves in West Palm Beach, Florida. There, the 30-year-old Shotkoski was taking an evening walk when a gunman demanded his money. Shotkoski refused. Shot twice, he managed to stagger some 300 feet to a busy street before collapsing near the curb.

Indicted for Shotkoski's murder was Neal Douglas Evans, a career criminal who, despite 13 previous convictions for robberies, burglaries, theft and drug possession, had slip-slided past forgiving judges for years. Because of a judicial order to relieve alleged overcrowding in Florida prisons, Evans was on his fourth so-called conditional release when he was charged with killing Shotkoski.

"I just don't understand," Felicia Shotkoski said when she learned that a habitual felon had been charged with her husband's murder.

I sympathize wholly with her. But after more than ten years studying America's criminal-justice system, I understand all too well. My research in crime statistics shows:

• Up to a *third* of those convicted of murder across the country were on parole, probation, or some other form of release at the time they took another person's life.

• Crime in general is getting more violent. Over the past three decades, your chances of becoming a crime victim increased 280 percent. But your chances of becoming a victim of violent crime increased 460 percent.

• The crime problem is bad enough, but demographic evidence indicates that it's going to get much worse.

Ordinary Americans feel that the criminal-justice system too often comes down on the side of the offender. Yet an influential

[4]Article by John J. DiIulio, Jr., director of The Brookings Institution Center for Public Management, from *Reader's Digest* 147/880:55-61 Aug '95. Copyright © 1995 by The Reader's Digest Assn., Inc. Reprinted with permission.

anti-incarceration lobby—including organizations such as the
National Council on Crime and Delinquency and the American
Civil Liberties Union—laments that our system is too harsh.

Whose instincts are correct? My research has convinced me
that the public is right. Statistics on computer printouts may not
show the blood on the sidewalk in West Palm Beach, but they confirm what people suspect about crime:

1. *The "declining crime rate" is misleading.* Much has been made
in the media over a 3 percent annual reduction during the past
three years in the number of crimes reported by police to the FBI.
It's too early to celebrate victory. Crime rates are still many times
higher today than they were in the 1950s, '60s, or '70s. And large
numbers of serious crimes today go unreported and unpunished.

In 1993, for example, the total number of crimes recorded
by the FBI was 14,141,000. But the FBI uses a method of
"hierarchical" counting in which only the "most serious" criminal
act in any one incident is reported. If a woman is raped and her
car stolen, for example, the FBI records the rape but not the
theft.

In contrast, the Justice Department's Bureau of Justice Statistics conducts a massive, ongoing survey. In 1993, for example,
more than 115,000 people in nearly 60,000 households were interviewed for information on crime. Their replies led to the estimate that the actual number of rapes, robberies, assaults,
burglaries and other crimes suffered by Americans in 1993 was
43,622,000—more than three times the FBI's number.

Moreover, the impact of crime is even worse if you live or
work in an urban area. My hometown, Philadelphia, is proof that
poor, minority and inner-city Americans (like my late grand-
mother, who was mugged three times) suffer the most from
crime.

In 1994, Philadelphia experienced over 400 murders. More
than 90 percent of the victims under age 20 were nonwhite. The
city's overall murder rate was 25.9 per 100,000 residents. But in
high-crime neighborhoods the murder rate is four times as high.

2. *Criminals are more violent.* A new breed of felon is "more terrorist than criminal," says a veteran bank robber who has spent
most of his last 30 years behind bars. In an alarming number of
cases, routine property crimes escalate into violent ones. This
past January in Atlanta, for instance, robbers who stole about
$100 in cash from two car rental agencies shot and killed three
unarmed men.

Violent crime has increased steadily over the past seven years. Well over 100,000 murders have been committed since the start of 1990. From 1985 through '93, while the murder rate by adults 25 and over dropped about 20 percent, it increased by 65 percent among 18- to 24-year-olds, and soared a terrifying 165 percent among 14- to 17-year-olds!

The current trend in birth rates makes it certain that a new violent crime wave is just around the corner. Today there are some 7.5 million males ages 14 through 17. By the year 2000 we will have an additional 500,000. About six percent of young males are responsible for half the serious crimes committed by their age group, studies reveal. Thus, in a few years we can expect at least 30,000 more murderers, rapists, robbers, and muggers on the streets than we have today.

Not long ago, I asked a group of long- and life-term prisoners what was triggering the explosion of violence among these new young criminals. I didn't hear the conventional explanations such as poverty or joblessness. Instead, these hardened men cited the absence of people—family, adults, teachers, preachers, coaches—who would care enough about young males to discipline them. In the vacuum, drug dealers and "gangsta rappers" serve as role models. "I was a bad-ass street gladiator," one prisoner told me, "but these kids are stone-cold predators."

3. *Our criminal-justice system is not handing down sentences to fit the crimes.* Most violent crimes go unreported, unprosecuted and unpunished. For example, in 1992 over 6.6 million violent crimes were committed, but just 3.3 million were reported to the police. About 641,000 led to arrests, barely 165,000 to convictions, and only 100,000 or so to prison sentences, which on average ended before the convict had served even half his time behind bars.

How often have you heard or read some variant of the claim that the United States has the highest incarceration rate in the world? We have more inmates per capita than other nations—but the appropriate measure is the rate of incarceration relative to the number of serious crimes. Here we are nowhere near to leading the pack. In fact, "hard time" for hardened criminals is rare.

Thanks to plea bargaining, hardened criminals often are able to "customize" their sentences. More than 90 percent of all defendants convicted of felonies had not gone to trial, but pleaded guilty to lesser charges. In Dade County, Florida, police detective Evelyn Gort was shot and killed by Wilbur Mitchell. Consider his previous record: despite nine felony convictions, he had been permitted to plea-bargain a sentence for auto theft down to one year and was released in less than four months. Had he served the full year, he would have been in prison the night he killed Gort.

Failing to incarcerate hardened criminals, or letting them go free too early, means more crimes of all kinds. Those convicted of homicide who were released from prison in 1992 had served, on average, only 5.9 years on sentences of 12.4 years.

Another sobering example of how the scales are tipping: In 1991 there were 590,000 probationers and parolees who had been convicted of a violent crime yet were residing in our communities. At the same time how many persons convicted of violent crimes were in prison? Only 372,000. Nearly half of criminals with one violent felony conviction are not sentenced to prison.

4. *Our prisons are not overcrowded with petty criminals and first-time drug offenders.* Again and again, the anti-incarceration lobby floats the notion that our prisons are overflowing with "first-timers" whose records show no history of violence. Most of these felons could be released tomorrow, it is argued, with little harm to society.

What are the facts? *Ninety-four* percent of state prisoners have been convicted of a violent crime such as murder, rape, robbery or assault, or are repeat criminal offenders, the U.S. Bureau of Justice Statistics reports.

Most adult prisoners are walking icebergs of crime, with the mass of their criminal records hidden beneath the surface. In extensive surveys I conducted of inmates in New Jersey and Wisconsin, half admitted committing 12 or more non-drug-related crimes in the year before they entered prison. These are conservative estimates; other reliable studies suggest that prisoners commit between 13 and 21 crimes a year when on the loose.

It is sometimes claimed that most prisoners now serving time for drug crimes—particularly those in the federal system—are in for mere possession. False. For example, only 703 of the 14,564 drug offenders newly committed to federal prisons in 1991 were convicted of possession. The other 96 percent were convicted of drug trafficking and other drug crimes. A recent survey found that the average quantity of drugs involved in their cases was 183 pounds for cocaine traffickers and 3.5 tons for marijuana.

5. *Despite "truth in sentencing" laws and get-tough rhetoric, too many convicts are still out on the streets.* Almost three-quarters of the five million felons under "correctional supervision" in 1993 were *not* incarcerated. They were somewhere out in the community, getting treatment for drug addiction, doing community service, or on parole or probation.

Today, most convicted criminals never see the inside of a prison. Instead, they are placed on probation. Then, within three years, nearly half abscond or are convicted of a new crime. Recently, a New York man suspected of terrorizing women with a string of sex attacks turned out to be a convicted rapist, released for "good behavior." He had been "dutifully checking in with his parole officer and even attending required rape counseling sessions," according to the New York *Times.*

Ongoing studies of many jurisdictions show that up to one in three murderers were "in custody" but out of jail—that is, on parole, pretrial release or probation—at the time they committed murder. From 1990 through '93, for instance, Virginia convicted 1411 people of murder, 33.5 percent of whom were "in custody" at the time of the crime.

One of those convicted was James Albert Steele III, who had shot a teenager in the face during a robbery attempt. Sentenced to ten years for that crime, he was out on parole when he shot and killed a Baptist minister at a bakery thrift store in Richmond. Steele then embarked on a night on the town with the dead man's car and $834 from the store's cash register.

We are making some progress in the battle to protect society from repeat offenders. Response to public outrage has resulted in tougher sentencing laws, and more attention is being focused on revolving-door justice. But we still have a long way to go.

From 1980 to 1992, the ten states where incarceration increased the most saw violent crime decrease by 8 percent. In the ten states with the lowest increases, violent crime soared 51 percent.

The dividends from imprisonment are huge—in lives preserved, property protected, order maintained. A study published in the journal *Science* calculated that in 1989 alone the increased use of imprisonment spared Americans an estimated 66,000 rapes, 323,000 robberies, 380,000 assaults, and 3.3 million burglaries. The Santa Monica-based research organization RAND estimated that California's new three-strikes law (life without parole for thrice-convicted felons) would prevent about 340,000 serious crimes per year.

The economic benefits are also substantial. Several studies show that for every dollar we spend to keep a serious criminal behind bars, we save ourselves at least two to three. The $16,000 to $25,000 a year it takes to incarcerate a felon is in fact a bargain, when balanced against the social costs of the crimes he would commit if free. Those costs include physical injuries, days missed from work, lost tax revenue, property damage, medical expenses and increased insurance premiums. A study published in the journal *Health Affairs* reported that each murder costs society $2.4 million, each rape $60,000, and each assault $22,000.

More incarceration will not prevent all crime, but it will bring a sense of order and justice to places where violent criminals prey freely on the innocent. And it will help check the next crime wave tied to the growing number of young predators.

REDRAWING THE FACE OF CRIME[5]

National surveys suggest that when many Americans think about crime, they see the face of a black jobless high-school dropout from a broken home.

In fact, the reality of crime is much different than that image, according to a new Department of Justice survey of more than 20,000 federal and state prison inmates released [April 1995] . . . in Washington, D.C.

Federal researchers found, for example, that many prisoners are reasonably well-educated. More than six out of 10 prisoners are high school graduates, and many attended college.

A majority of federal prison inmates and nearly half of all state prisoners are white or white Hispanic, not African American. More than four out of 10 prisoners were raised in two-parent families, and more than half had full-time jobs before their arrest.

[5]Article by Lester Brown, from *Society* 32/4:2-3 My/Ju '95. Copyright © 1995 by Transaction Publishers. Reprinted with permission.

That's not to say that broken homes, joblessness, and a medio-cre education aren't enormous risk factors. They are, and likely always will be. But these new numbers suggest that solutions to the crime problem lie well beyond the simplistic, single-short so-lutions ("three strikes and yer out!" comes immediately to mind), and give lie to some of the comfortable stereotypes that the aver-age American has about the causes of crime.

Here are some of the myths and near-myths about crime— and the reality, as revealed by the Justice study:

• Lack of education leads to crime. It's a warning that rings in the ears of children for a lifetime: Drop out of school and drop into a life of crime. The problem is, most state and federal prison-ers aren't high school dropouts. Nearly six out of 10 state prison inmates—59 percent—and more than three out of four federal prisoners—77 percent—have at least a high school education. In fact, 28 percent of all federal prisoners and 12 percent of state prison inmates attended at least some college.

• Broken homes lead to crime. It's true that children raised in single-parent households are disproportionately more likely to become involved in criminality than those who are not. But the survey revealed that 43 percent of state prison inmates and 58 percent of federal prisoners were raised by both parents.

• The face of crime is black. It is true that blacks are dispro-portionately represented in the overall prison populations in both state and federal facilities, relative to their proportion in the pop-ulation.

But the survey also suggests that fewer than half of all inmates in state prison are American-born blacks. In fact, there are signif-icantly more whites (38 percent) than blacks (30 percent) in feder-al prisons. In state penal facilities, 46 percent of the inmates are black, and 35 percent are white. Hispanics, who are mostly but not exclusively white, make up 28 percent of all federal prisoners and 17 percent of state inmates, the survey suggests, with other races comprising the remainder.

• Joblessness leads to crime. Again, no argument that unem-ployment is a considerable risk factor. But the Justice survey found that most prisoners were employed full-time before their arrest. According to the survey, 56 percent of those state prison-ers interviewed and 65 percent of the federal inmates had full-time jobs before they were arrested. About one out of 10 state and federal prisoners were employed part-time; only one out of six state and federal prisoners were classified as "discouraged workers"—unemployed and not looking for work. (Still, the data suggest these jobs were something less than lucrative: More than half of all prisoners reported pre-arrest annual incomes of less than $15,000 a year; a quarter of all federal prisoners and one out of seven state inmates earned $25,000 or more.)

Some caveats are in order. First, this survey is of prison inmates, and by definition does not include persons convicted of a crime and given probation, or sentenced to do jail time. And differences in the kinds of crimes prosecuted by state and federal governments—and the differences between the kinds of people who commit certain kinds of crime (securities fraud versus liquor store stickups, for example)—produces many of the differences between the two prison populations.

Federal inmates tended, on average, to be older (36 years versus 30 years), better-educated and generally more "white collar" than state prison inmates. Nearly half of all state prisoners were doing time for committing violent crimes, compared with 17 percent of all federal prisoners. Federal inmates were, however, twice as likely to be in for drug violations. And significantly, federal prisoners expected to serve more of their sentences than did state prisoners.

The survey also showed that most inmates were experienced drug users. Six out of 10 federal prisoners and eight out of 10 state inmates said they had used illicit drugs sometime in their lives. Nearly a third of all state prisoners said they were on drugs at the time they committed the crime that resulted in their incarceration, compared with 17 percent of all federal prisoners. And one out of six state prisoners and one out of 10 federal inmates said they committed the crime "to get money for drugs."

One out of four state prisoners but nearly four out of 10 state prison inmates said they had a relative who had been in prison.

A random sampling of 14,000 state prisoners and 6,600 federal inmates were interviewed in 1991 for the study, which was jointly sponsored by the Bureau of Justice Statistics and the Federal Bureau of Prisons.

STANDING UP TO VIOLENCE[6]

The premature death of young James Darby, the 9-year-old New Orleans boy who was shot in the head during a drive-by shooting as he walked home from a Mother's Day picnic last spring, was, at the time, just the latest in a long progression of heartbreaking stories marking an American childhood world that seems to have gone mad with vicious and random violence.

"I want you to stop the killing in the city," the youngster had desperately pleaded in a letter to President Clinton just nine days before his murder. "I think someone might kill me. I'm asking you nicely to stop it. I know you can do it."

Young James was both prophetically right and understandably wrong in his plea. He was right that violence in his city, indeed in almost every U.S. city and in many suburbs and towns as well, threatens tens of thousands of children and teenagers with bodily and psychological harm. And he was right that this societal sickness would soon claim him as well. As we all know, danger and fear stalk too many of our homes, streets, and schools, and— more than any other group—children and teenagers are its victims, as well as its perpetrators.

But James was wrong in thinking that the "most powerful man in the world"—even acting with the full force of government— could stop the scourge of violence that is cutting short so many young lives. It will take a far more profound and widespread response than any President can muster to end this latest social plague that deprives so many young people of life, liberty, and the pursuit of happiness.

Following James' death, President Clinton wrote his classmates, trying to console them: "I am deeply saddened to learn of his tragic death, and I assure each of you that I'm determined to answer James' plea with tough and smart solutions to the crime problems in America."

The President then invoked James Darby's tragic tale as he pressed the Congress to end six years of partisan bickering and

[6]Article by R. Craig Sautter, writer, editor, and teacher at the School for New Learning at DePaul University, from the January 1995 issue of *Phi Delta Kappan* 76/ 5:1-12. Copyright © 1995 by *Phi Delta Kappan*. Reprinted with permission.

pass his omnibus crime bill. The final version of the bill included $5 billion for youth programs. But two-thirds of the "pork" cut in the final congressional debate came from funds that would have been directed to youth.

Even with the President's signature on this bill, though, the task of once more making the world safe for and from young people will be a long and arduous one. Many law enforcement officials, while pleased to get additional help, are skeptical about the ultimate impact of the law on crime—and particularly on youth crime.

"The current crime bill and its 'more police on the streets and more prisons' approach is not likely to have the effects that they are selling," confides an FBI agent who works with the public schools and young people in Washington, D.C. "Congress has been passing similar crime bills since Nixon was in office more than 20 years ago, and it obviously hasn't had much impact. There are already three times as many people in jail as 15 years ago. The problem starts at home and in the community. Not enough people care about the things they should care about," he argues.

Carnage in the Streets

Every two days, guns kill the equivalent of a class of 25 youngsters and injure 60 more, according to the Children's Defense Fund, which has a memorable way of presenting statistics. Adolescents between the ages of 10 and 19 are killed with a gun at a rate of one every three hours. In fact, an American child today is 15 times more likely to be killed by gunfire than was a child in war-ravaged Northern Ireland before the recent peace talks.

Every year since 1950, the number of American children gunned down has doubled. Today homicide is the third leading cause of death for all children between the ages of 5 and 14, the second leading cause of death for all young people between the ages of 10 and 24, and the leading cause of death among African Americans of both sexes between the ages of 15 and 34. Teenagers are more than 2½ times as likely to be victims of violent crime as are those over 20 years of age.

Although no long, black granite wall commemorates them in our nation's capital, more U.S. young people have been killed by guns in their own homeland during the last 13 years than lost their lives in Vietnam during that quarter-century war! (The closest thing to a monument for these youngsters was the chilling collection of 80,000 empty shoes spread across the Capitol Hill mall this fall, relics of adult and youthful victims of gun violence.)

Yet the American public—numbed by decades of television, radio, newspaper, and real-life images of dehumanizing violence—has not responded to the loss of so many children and teenagers with the same sorrow, anger, or grief as was roused by Vietnam. Fortunately, that situation may be changing, as some adults are beginning to say, "Enough is enough," and candle-light vigils and marches are becoming more common as communities grope for solutions.

Juvenile Victimization

Anthropologically speaking, violence seems almost endemic to the human species, something civilization is constantly struggling to suppress. (Violence is generally defined as injurious or homicidal action toward others.) "History is a slaughterhouse," the 19th-century German philosopher Hegel declared. Our own century has done little to prove him wrong. In the contemporary world, over a million people are murdered or commit suicide each year.

In the U.S. more than 20,000 people die each year from violent acts, while another 2.2 million are injured. Incredibly, more than 10,000 young people between the ages of 10 and 24 are murdered or commit suicide (violence against themselves) each year. Over half of the people arrested for murder in the U.S. in 1991 were under the age of 25.

Still, our culture of violence is romanticized in our history and in our entertainment. In the midst of a youth murder epidemic, a film like *Natural Born Killer[s]* becomes a nationwide sensation, and its soundtrack blares from teenagers' boom boxes. Our culture of violence has spawned the children of violence, even child murderers, and suddenly we seem shocked.

In July 1994 the U.S. Department of Justice released a report noting that the number of violent crimes perpetrated against juveniles between the ages of 12 and 17 had risen nearly 24% between 1988 and 1992. "Although juveniles accounted for one-tenth of the population age 12 and over," the report observed, "nearly one in four violent crimes involved a juvenile victim in

1992—up from one in five in 1987." About one in 13 youngsters is now victimized. Compare that to a ratio of one in 35 for adults over 35 years of age. During the same years the raw numbers rose from 5.8 million to 6.2 million young victims. Six out of 10 crimes against young people were assaults.

The problem is complicated by the 211 million firearms circulating among the American public. There are more gun dealers in the United States (284,000) than gas stations. Youth gangs have discovered that it isn't too difficult to go into the arms business along with the drug business. Just as the U.S. government is the biggest arms merchant on the world scene, so the nation's youth gangs now see the enormous profits in the small arms business.

Most observers agree that the easy availability of firearms is clearly a contributing factor to the unacceptable level of youth murder that haunts our communities. "Back in the 1970s when I defended kids in court, I wouldn't have five kids with guns in a year," says Judge Susan Larabee of the Bronx Family Court in New York City. "Now almost every single case I see involves not just a gun, but a loaded gun."

Although public opinion is shifting, legislative moves against guns are decried as unconstitutional. While more laws may help and strict enforcement would help even more, new laws are clearly not the answer. Most states already prohibit juveniles from carrying handguns and automatic weapons, but these laws have made little difference in the past. To solve this problem, society must devise strategies to find and disarm kids with guns.

Meanwhile, some children who become violent are not safe in their own homes and are regularly victimized by the adults entrusted to care for them. There is a direct and indisputable connection between violence in the home or against children in the home and subsequent violent behavior by those children. Psychologists confirm that children exposed to violence are sometimes as traumatized as children in war zones. For many youngsters, their American childhood has literally become a war zone in which they are entrapped—forced to run for cover and to avoid playgrounds, front yards, neighborhood streets, and even their own homes.

Psychological Impact

In some places where American children grow up, gunfire rattles on and on, day and night. Many inner-city youngsters go to more funerals than movies and are scarred for years thereafter by the violence they have witnessed.

The violence inflicted on our young takes more than a physical toll. The American Psychological Association reports that the post-traumatic stress that children experience as either victims of or witnesses to violence "includes intrusive imagery, emotional constriction or avoidance, fears of recurrence, sleep difficulties, disinterest in significant activities, and attention difficulties."All of these interfere with normal development, with learning in school, and with living a happy childhood. Thus violence endures deep in the psyches of children long after their immediate victimization.

Because so much violence these days seems random, everyone is affected in some way. As the mass media dramatize youth crime incessantly on the evening news and create hyper-crime for the core of the entertainment industry, the real fear that accompanies the cumulative damage of real murders and assaults perpetrated by and upon young people is greatly magnified, becoming pervasive, perplexing, and paralyzing to the society at large. For example, one Northwestern University study found that three-fifths of local Chicago news time was devoted to coverage of violence, a factor that surely contributes to the public paranoia about violence.

Even when danger may be remote, it seems ever-present. From watching news reports and the prime-time violence blitz, we illogically conclude that, because someone is in danger somewhere, everyone must be in jeopardy all the time. While the danger to many youths is all too real, to others it is all too exaggerated, insidiously warping social relationships and community life.

Some experts estimate that as little as 1% of the general population will exhibit regular violent behavior. If that figure is accurate, that means that 99% of the people are terrorized by a minuscule minority. But the entire society is held hostage, and that violent minority, when armed and angry, inflicts a heavy toll on those in their way.

Is It Worse Than Ever?

Historically speaking, how bad is contemporary youth crime? How much of the phenomenon of youth violence is merely hype aimed at arousing fear and dread?

Overall, the United States has the highest homicide rate in the industrial world. The nation recorded 23,760 murders in 1992, which makes homicide the 10th most common cause of death. In 1993, 22 cities set murder records. Clearly, crime in America seems much higher than a decade and a half ago, when experts say the latest wave of mayhem began with the appearance of crack and kids with guns.

According to one *New York Times* estimate, crime is up more than 600% since the 1950s. But is the problem of youth crime and violence worse than ever? Is this the most violent generation to enter our society, as some suggest? Or is the magnification of the media, which focus on the most spectacular crimes, creating a distorted hysteria that only promotes more violence among youth?

Statistics vary from source to source—but, according to FBI arrest figures, the public perception that more young people are in trouble with the law than ever before is statistically *incorrect*. Surprisingly, in both gross numbers and percentage of all crime, youth crime hit its high point in the mid-1970s. Since then the number of youth arrests has fallen significantly. However, the kinds of crime that young people commit are more serious today than in the past, and youthful criminals are becoming younger and younger. Moreover, youth homicide is worse than ever.

Delinquents: 1940s to 1970s

Youth crime first became a national issue more than half a century ago. "The problem of juvenile delinquency, as President Truman has affirmed, is of serious concern to the whole country," wrote Ralph Banay in *Youth in Despair* back in 1948.

"All intelligent Americans face the challenge of a dismaying, ever-increasing rise in the rate of crime—and in its tremendous costs, whether cost is reckoned in dollars and cents or in social disintegration," Banay declared. "The core of the crime problem is the great and still growing question of errant youth. Well over 20% of all crime is charged to our young people: a fact implicit with accusations pointed toward the forces charged with inspiring and protecting youth—our schools, churches, local governments, and homes." Sound familiar?

In America's pop culture imagination, the 1950s were the decade of "juvenile delinquency," particularly in movies with such scary titles as *Blackboard Jungle*, which seemed to depict a real problem. But the difference between then and now is the simple fact that guns have replaced fists and switchblades.

By 1960 the total number of youths arrested still seemed relatively tame. But statistics for that year provide a point of reference for today's youth violence. In 1960 those 18 and under accounted for 633,720 arrests or about 17% of all arrests. A reported 513 of those arrests were for murder and nonnegligent homicide; 10,155, for robbery; 7,678, for assault; and 1,763, for drug offenses.

The real explosion in youth crime began in 1970, when 1,660,643 people under the age of 18 were arrested—about 26% of all arrests that year. Of these, 1,346 arrests were for murder, a number that had more than doubled in five years; arrests for robbery tripled to 29,289; 20,756 arrests were for assault; and drug-related arrests soared to 77,756. (Remember that the violent images of the Vietnam War were still making nightly intrusions into American homes via the family television set. And during the 1970s the U.S. suffered some difficult economic jolts and accompanying social changes.)

By 1975 total arrests for youths 18 and under vaulted to 2,078,459, holding steady at about 26% of all arrests. Youth arrests for murder reached 1,578; for robbery, 44,470; for assault, 35,612; and for drug-related offenses, 122,857.

But contrary to popular opinion, youth arrests did not continue to climb as dramatically in the 1980s and early 1990s as in the 1970s. Arrests of young people 18 and younger actually fell to 2,025,713 in 1980, dropping to 20% of all arrests. Yet arrests of young people for murder continued to climb (to 1,742); arrests for robbery fell to 41,997; arrests for assault increased to 38,135; and drug-related arrests fell to 100,688.

Significant Declines

By 1990 the youth arrest rate actually plunged to 15% of all arrests or 1,754,542, down from the all-time high of 26% in 1975 and even below the 1960 percentage. (The nation's population is much larger in 1990, so total numbers are larger.) The data from 1992, the most recent year for which complete FBI arrest statistics are available, indicate that the total youth arrest rate in that year had climbed one percentage point to 16% of all arrests or a total of 1,943,138 arrests, still far below the 1975 peak.

But 2,829 youths under age 18 were arrested for murder in 1992, a frightening statistic that continues to scare everyone and to make the issue of youth violence critically important. In 1992, 40,434 young people were arrested for robbery; 63,777, for assault; and 73,981, for drug offenses.

Hence the percentage of youth arrests against all arrests, as reported by the FBI, is now lower than it was two decades ago. The perception that this generation of young people is more violent than ever in terms of raw numbers is suspect, if not simply false. In fact, all U.S. crime is at a 20-year low (35.7 million crimes in 1973 versus 33.6 million in 1992.) However, 1992 was a record-setting year for violent crimes committed with a handgun. And, according to the Department of Justice, young black males between the ages of 20 and 24 are now three times more likely to be victims of gun violence than young white males.

Statistics aside, things are very bad for many, but not all, kids. Too many youngsters are injured or killed, too many families are devastated, and too many wayward youths have their lives ruined by crime and incarceration. And the yearly toll, higher or lower statistically, continues to accumulate. Hence, after a decade, the number of dead children and teenagers amounts to an incredible toll that statistics do not begin to address.

A New Kind of Youth Violence

What is worse than ever in the 1990s is the youth murder rate, coupled with the diminishing age of many perpetrators. Apparently, more children are becoming more violent at earlier ages, and they are committing more violent crimes, often repeatedly, before they even have a chance to become teenagers.

"The kids I see come from such violent homes and backgrounds," reports Judge Larabee. "They may have a brother or two in jail for a violent crime. There may be mental illness in the family. There has probably been domestic violence. They may have had a father or mother shot or murdered. Many of these kids are already third-generation violent offenders. Their whole lives are surrounded by violence. They play violent video games. I've had two cases where kids were playing video games, went out and murdered someone, and went back to play more video games. There is no difference for them between 'Mortal Combat' and real life."

According to some psychologists, the intensity of today's youth violence is also greater than it was a few years ago. The viciousness and the casualness of the violent crimes committed by and against youths are especially troubling.

Some social critics charge that this new kind of violence means that respect for life, the bedrock of any ethical social system, is no longer sacred. For example, a survey by Joseph Skeley and M. Dwayne Smith of Tulane University found that 20% of students at one suburban high school saw nothing wrong with shooting someone who had stolen something from them. The researchers also discovered a greater willingness among today's teens to "pull the trigger." And they concluded that today's gun violence is not necessarily linked to drugs. They speculated that larger social forces may be at work.

What happens to the kids who are arrested? Nationally, one-third of young people accused of violent acts remain in custody. That means that two-thirds of these youngsters go on probation or are set free. Only 3% are tried in adult courts. Moreover, even juveniles found guilty of murder can be held only in juvenile facilities until they are 21 years of age. In most states, these facilities are filled to capacity and are unable to offer the intensive help these youngsters require.

In addition, violent youths have a 70% recidivism rate, although some studies indicate that graduates of the boot camps seem to have just a 50% recidivism rate. In either case, many crimes committed by young people are the work of repeat offenders.

California, Florida, and nearly 20 other states have introduced or passed legislation to stiffen laws governing juveniles. But it may prove far easier—and ultimately more effective—to target these kids early on, when they first exhibit violent behavior, than to spend a lifetime being victimized by them and subsequently punishing them in expensive and hopeless penal institutions. This approach would nonetheless require a commitment to intensive intervention on the part of a community that wants to protect itself in the future.

Schools in the Crossfire

Over three million assorted crimes—about 11% of all crimes—occur each year in America's 85,000 public schools. That compares with one million crimes each year in America's workplaces. In fact, a school crime takes place every six seconds. Some critics charge that figures for school crime are significantly underreported, because schools treat many incidents as discipline problems rather than as crimes.

While the popular perception is that school crime is primarily an urban problem, a 1991 report from the U.S. Justice Department, *School Crime: A National Crime Victimization Survey Report*, indicates otherwise. It found that suburban and urban students are about equally victimized. The report concluded that 2% of students from both settings and 1% of rural students were victims of violent crime, such as assault, robbery, and rape. The study polled 10,000 students between the ages of 12 and 19. Projecting those figures to the entire student population meant that approximately 430,000 students were victims of violent crime. The Justice Department also found that 13% of high school seniors had been threatened with a weapon.

The similarity in crime statistics between cities and suburbs might be attributed to the fact that urban districts have dealt with the problem for some time and have some workable intervention strategies in place. For example, urban schools are more likely to use hall monitors and metal detectors, so some problems are kept in the neighborhoods and out of the schools. Many urban school districts, such as San Diego and Houston, have adopted "zero tolerance" on guns and weapons. And in late October, President Clinton announced an executive order directing the states to require all school districts to enact the "zero tolerance" policy by expelling for one year any student who brings a gun to school. A conference committee had cut the measure out of the legislation reauthorizing the Elementary and Secondary Education Act. Federal funds can be cut off from states that fail to comply.

While schools secure their buildings and grounds, it is essential to understand that violent youths who are expelled must be reached in other ways or they will simply wreak havoc somewhere else. In the big cities, where dropout rates are high, the violence against students is often perpetrated by nonstudents. Turning more students out on the streets without providing the intensive help they need will not solve the larger problem.

Metal detectors seem prudent because national estimates are that more than 200,000 students pack weapons along with their school lunches and bring them into the learning environment every day, destabilizing classes, terrorizing teachers and peers, and often killing teachers, administrators, and other students. According to the National School Safety Center, last year guns led to 35 deaths and 92 injuries in the schools. Moreover, other lives are ruined in the cluster of social ramifications that any death brings to those associated with both the victim and the killer.

A Justice Department study found that 22% of inner-city boys own guns. According to researchers at the University of Michigan, 9% of eighth-graders nationally carry a gun, knife, or club to school at least once a month. The Michigan researchers estimated that students carry 270,000 guns to school each day. And the National Education Association calculates that on any given day about 160,000 students stay home because of fear of violence in or on the way to school. Indeed, their fear may be warranted: firearms are the fourth leading cause of accidental death among children between the ages of 5 and 14.

"Guns just make it too easy to kill people," explains Judge Larabee. "There is no personal involvement between the killer and the victim. It's between them and the gun and has almost nothing to do with the other kids. That's why so many kids 'accidentally' kill their best friends. The semiautomatics make it easier because you hardly have to aim."

Getting Worse

While the rate of juvenile arrests may be down from two decades ago, school violence is worse now than it was five years ago, according to 75% of the 700 school districts that participated in a 1994 national survey of suburban, urban, and rural schools, conducted by the National School Boards Association (NSBA). The group concluded that two factors—the disintegration of the family and the increasing depiction of violence in the media and in popular music—are the leading causes of violence in public schools. Other contributing causes, according to the NSBA, are alcohol and drug abuse, easy access to guns, and poverty.

"The problem of school violence cannot be solved by schools working alone," said Thomas Shannon, NSBA executive director. "It will require intensive efforts by the entire community to reduce the epidemic of violence in the nation's schools."

The NSBA survey found that student assaults against other students, students bringing weapons to the classroom, student attacks on teachers, racial and ethnic violence, and gang-related problems were the top five types of violent incidents reported in schools during 1993. Nearly 40% of urban districts reported shootings or knife attacks, while 23% experienced drive-by shootings.

It is not just individual victims who suffer from school crime. All students are victimized by the fear, the anger, the guilt, the anguish, and the sense of helplessness that follow an act of school violence. A 1994 Gallup poll found that two-thirds of all teenagers said their "best friends" had been physically harmed in the last 12 months. However, another study by the National Center for Education Statistics found that only 8% of high school sophomores feel unsafe in their schools, down from 12% in 1980.

"Many of the youth we surveyed are being denied a fundamental sense of security," says Mark Singer, associate professor at the Mandel School of Applied Social Sciences, Case Western Reserve University. Singer surveyed 3,700 teenagers in Ohio and Colorado. More than half of the Cleveland high school students in the survey had witnessed knife attacks or stabbings. One-third of the students in a small Ohio town had witnessed the same behavior. Over half of the boys in the survey had perpetrated some form of violence during the preceding year, such as punching, hitting, or slapping someone. Among girls, sexual abuse was higher in the small towns than in the big cities in the survey.

"Many individuals in this survey have been exposed to significant levels of violence and are at risk of developing serious, long-term problems as a result," Singer concluded.

Sources of Youth Violence

Seventeen hundred years ago, the Roman emperor and Stoic philosopher Marcus Aurelius observed that "poverty is the mother of crime." His insight endures because it is at least partially true. For the past 25 years, child welfare experts have warned that the grinding poverty, inequitable educational opportunity, latchkey homes, child abuse, domestic violence, and family breakups, as well as the general abandonment of children to a constant barrage of televised mayhem, would result in escalating real-world violence. Those predictions were pretty much ignored, while everyone blamed everyone else and the condition of children and teenagers continued to decline.

Others warn that today's problem is just the beginning. "Unless we fix our schools and give these kids opportunities, this current wave of violence will look like a picnic in comparison to the gangs and violence we will have in the future," predicts Joe Kellman, co-founder of the innovative Corporate/Community School in Chicago. He sees little inclination toward or progress in developing social supports because he believes that those in control of national resources are indifferent to the problem, if not cynically racist about who is getting killed.

Despite our sophistication, despite a pledge to end poverty 25 years ago, and despite the nation's more recent commitment to get children "ready to learn" before they enter school, U.S. society continues to allow nearly a quarter of its young people to grow up in such desperate and degrading material conditions that the struggle of daily survival can warp the human spirit and deaden moral consciousness. Year after year this psychic destruction of children goes on, waylaying more and more millions of young people.

Obviously, not all poor children respond to the conditions of their lives with destructive anger and aggression. Many use poverty as a motivation for success. And it is unfair, indeed prejudicial, to characterize urban youth as violent youth. In fact, much of today's mayhem is the unexpected and nihilistic work of troubled middle-class youngsters. But that's no surprise either. The typical U.S. child of any ethnic or economic group has witnessed more than 8,000 murders and hundreds of thousands of acts of violence on television by the time he or she leaves eighth grade. One recent study by Sen. Byron Dorgan (D-N.D.) recorded 1,000 violent acts on television each week. Without critical lenses to filter this barrage of antisocial behavior, children begin to have unreal and destructive social expectations and desires.

Yet in more and more urban and suburban neighborhoods, kids are afraid to ride their bikes lest they become victims of a drive-by shooting or an assault. In the course of writing this article, I interrupted two separate incidents in which young children were thrown to the ground and viciously kicked in the head by youths their own age or a little older. One took place on a city street next to a decrepit school, the other in an affluent schoolyard far from the threat of urban street gangs.

No wonder many mothers are forced to keep their children cooped up in apartments or homes. Unfortunately, as a result, most youngsters spend their time watching the cartoon violence on their television sets. In fact, Americans spend 97% of their time indoors. Many do so because they are afraid to go outside.

Psychological Roots

The reduction of youth crime in general may be partially the result of the thousands of anti-violence and mediation courses that have been in place in America's schools since 1972. But the new kind of violence we are seeing suggests that real remedies need to be more specialized and better focused than is generally acknowledged. Teaching students mediation skills, for example, although a good strategy to help many kids cope socially, is not likely to prevent the worst kinds of crimes by children who show early signs of violent behàvior. These young people need to be identified quickly and given professional help to learn how to work out their problems in socially permissible ways.

In response to the disturbing and complicated problem of youth violence, the American Psychological Association (APA) has launched a number of studies, new programs, and media outreach efforts that will continue over the next few years. Its first report, *Violence & Youth: Psychology's Response*, is an overview of the APA's findings and provides a number of useful insights for teachers, parents, and communities working to confront the frightening situation of children killing children. The report reflects 50 years of research on child and teenage aggression and other related phenomena. For educators, many of its implications will suggest strategies for action that can be added to new or current school anti-violence plans.

The APA lists domestic violence, hate crimes, sexual violence, and peer violence as the leading threats to the safety of today's children and teenagers. But what causes a person to become violent? According to APA researchers, the causes are many and complex, ranging from "biological factors, child-rearing conditions, ineffective parenting, emotional and cognitive development, gender differences, sex role socialization, relations to peers, cultural milieu, social factors such as economic inequality and lack of opportunity, and media influences, among others."

The APA concluded that it is difficult to sort out the roles of heredity, biology (e.g., head trauma), and learned behavior. Indeed, some recent research by neuroscientists suggests that genetic "defects" that produce abnormal levels of two brain chemicals, serotonin and noradrenaline, may account for some violent behavior. The biology of violence is a subject that will be debated often in years to come.

On the positive side, the APA is confident that much of the social violence we are witnessing today is learned behavior. That leads to the APA's optimistic conclusion that, if violence is learned, it can be unlearned.

The Strongest Predictor

The APA found that "the strongest developmental predictor of a child's involvement in violence is a history of previous violence." That includes having been a victim of abuse. (About 70% of men who come through the criminal justice system were abused or neglected children.) The APA also found that "children who show a fearless, impulsive temperament very early in life may have a predisposition for aggression and violent behavior."

That is why the APA says that early childhood intervention to prevent future violence is "critical." Children who show signs of antisocial behavior need to be targeted early for school and family intervention, not only to teach them new ways to resolve social conflicts, but also to ensure that their aggressive tendencies do not interfere with their potential for educational achievement and so contribute to even greater social and learning problems later.

Preschools, Head Start programs, and the early elementary years are times when educators must have the skills and resources, as well as the assistance of psychologists and social workers, to thwart future problems of violence during the difficult years of adolescence. If we are serious about reducing violence, it is ridiculous to ignore the causes insofar as we know them. Therefore, early action is imperative.

Nor should popular remedies such as instruction in nonviolence and mediation be confined to the middle and high school years, when the problem has grown serious. The early years are the best time for schools to teach these skills, particularly if they are not being taught in the home.

Adult Abandonment

The APA confirms the popular notion that a "breakdown of family processes and relationships" contributes to "the development of antisocial behaviors, including violence." Poor families are not the only ones involved in this situation. Increasingly, families in all economic strata exhibit these problems. The APA found that "lack of parental supervision is one of the strongest predictors of the development of conduct problems and delinquency."

However, supervision does not mean overzealous punishment. The APA warned that "harsh and continual physical punishment by parents has been implicated in the development of aggressive behavior patterns." Conversely, it found that positive interactions by parents and other adults can lessen the risk of developing violent behavior. This is a conclusion also reached by "resilience researchers," who have found that the involvement of just one caring adult can make all the difference in the life of an "at-risk" youth. The first step toward creating real opportunities for young people is reintroducing adults from the community and other places into the lives of these youngsters.

Negative School Factors

As all teachers know, aggressive and disruptive behavior in the classroom often leads to poor school performance and destructive peer relationships, which in turn contribute to the "trajectory toward violence." The APA didn't blame schools, but it did find that several aspects of school organization "help create a milieu that is conducive to aggression." These include "high numbers of students occupying a small space"; the "imposition of behavioral routines and conformity" that may contribute to feelings of "anger, resentment, and rejection"; and poor building designs that "may facilitate the commission of violent acts."

Schools that are serious about reducing violent behavior need to analyze the dynamics of their own cultures to identify both sources of friction and ways in which children and teenagers are permitted—even encouraged—to express their emotions. For example, University of Minnesota researchers David Johnson and Roger Johnson argue that cooperative learning, in addition to contributing to academic improvement, also teaches social and mediation skills that enable young people to live in greater harmony.

Violence is not an inevitable response on the part of children and teenagers. The APA urged that, "on the positive side, early exposure to cultural influences that enable the child to build a positive ethnic identity and a sense of belonging to a group with shared traditions and values may help buffer the child against social risk factors for the involvement in violence."

Searching for Solutions

But what can schools that are caught in the crossfire of youth violence do to protect their students and to get at fundamental psychological and behavioral habits? A 1994 Honeywell survey of teachers and students, titled *Keeping Our Schools Safe*, found that 82% of teachers believed that parenting classes could help reduce violence, while 78%) recommended smaller classes, 77% called for stricter discipline, 72% called for more student involvement in discipline procedures, and 76% said that schools need family support systems. Only 30% of the teachers surveyed thought that metal detectors or more security guards could help the situation.

According to the NSBA, many schools are standing up to violence by trying everything from enacting new school suspension policies to using closed-circuit television on school buses and adopting "zero tolerance" policies for possession of weapons or for any kind of violent behavior. More than 70% of the districts in the NSBA survey collaborate with social service agencies to address underlying causes of violence. About 60% of the districts teach students the skills of conflict resolution and peer mediation. (Nationwide, more than 2,000 schools conduct conflict resolution programs.) Half of the districts surveyed reported that they search lockers, 41% have established dress codes, and 24% use drug-sniffing dogs on occasion. But only 15% of the districts in the NSBA survey use metal detectors in their schools. Other studies show that more than 45% of urban school systems use metal detectors.

The debate rages over whether or not metal detectors do the job. "There is little evidence that metal detectors work," says Ronald Stevens, president of the National School Safety Council. But 10% of more of the nation's 100 largest districts are using metal detectors this year than did so last year. Detroit schools installed them in 1985, New York City schools in 1987, and Kansas City, Missouri, schools in 1993.

The federal Centers for Disease Control and Prevention advise that metal detectors may reduce but won't eliminate gun violence. The centers concluded that the detectors "have no apparent effect on the number of injuries, deaths, or threats of violence" at schools. And they don't address long-term problems.

The Dallas Independent Schools have introduced a multifaceted strategy to reduce violence. The program has placed new campus safety teams at every school, consisting of specially trained teachers, counselors, and security people. Other components of the program include a crisis planning guide for principals, 24-hour hotlines for students to call in with confidential information, and peer mediation projects. The state of North Carolina started a Scholastic Crime Stoppers program that pays rewards of up to $1,000 for crime tips. The schools in Dade County, Florida, adopted the nation's first gun awareness program.

Indeed, hundreds of schools across the nation have also tried to confront the issue of violence by introducing anti-violence curricula, conflict resolution, and conflict management. Students learn a variety of options they can resort to instead of turning to violence. Some schools train as many as 50 student mediators to conduct hundreds of mediation sessions to resolve everyday disputes.

A five-year study by the National Institute on Drug Abuse and the National Institute of Mental Health found that one program—Anger Management for Youth: Stemming Aggression and Violence—did a good job of teaching ways to reduce anger. The study tracked 1,200 at-risk teenagers from Washington, D.C. After just five months, the students had fewer problems with anger, less depression, and fewer feelings of hopelessness and stress.

Many schools use the Resolving Conflict Creatively Program, which began as a partnership between the New York City schools and Educators for Social Responsibility. Forty schools in New York City participate in Project STOP (Schools Teaching Options for Peace).

Students who become mediators learn to listen, to act as role models, to initiate discussions, to channel feedback, to change personal habits, to be vigilant, to deal with their fear, to guide others, and to become learners. In general, teachers who work with students using mediation and resolution approaches feel that their students have more respect for one another, are more at ease, know alternatives they can pursue, and are able to think about the consequences of their actions. Adults say these programs get kids to take responsibility for maintaining behavioral standards.

But if they are to succeed, good mediation programs require lots of training for teachers and students. And they need to give authority to students to nominate the people they think will make the fairest mediators. Schools must make that commitment, or their efforts will be diluted from the beginning.

Conflict resolution training is now mandated by the state of Illinois. Minnesota has allocated nearly $2.5 million for violence prevention education and has developed a progressive statewide plan for integrating its violence reduction program into the general curriculum. At Coventry Elementary School in Cleveland Heights, Ohio, peace is a unifying theme of learning and living together. Even first-graders are taught mediation skills.

Thinking the Problem Through

Counteracting youth violence requires more than a criminal justice approach, and scores of new anti-violence curricula have been developed over the past decade. One new approach comes from Ronald Slaby, a senior scientist at the Education Development Center in Newton, Massachusetts, who is also a member of the APA Commission on Youth and Violence. Along with colleagues Renée Wilson-Brewer and Kim Dash, Slaby developed a new middle school curriculum called *Aggressors, Victims, and Bystanders: Thinking and Acting to Prevent Violence.* The 12-session curriculum, funded by a grant from the federal Centers for Disease Control and Prevention, will be one of the teaching modules for teenagers that are distributed through the health departments of all 50 states.

"Violence is learned, so it can be unlearned, or not learned at all," Slaby asserts. "You can change your habits of thinking. The truth is that kids can do it easier than adults." But young people have to be taught how to think of alternatives, clearly and specifically, Slaby reasons. Then they have to practice their new behavior. His curriculum is designed "to teach a think-first model," in which students go through four steps.

1. *Keeping cool.* They talk about being cool-headed versus hot-headed. (The terms were chosen based on feedback from the participants.)

2. *Sizing up the situation.* This step is important because the way young people define a problem influences the solutions they pick. Slaby explains that violent offenders define a problem in hostile ways and automatically treat other people as adversaries when that may not be warranted.

3. *Thinking it through.* Kids learn to think of alternative solutions, as well as to think about the consequences. "Violent juvenile offenders simply do not think things through," says Slaby. "Ironically, our jails are filled with youngsters and even adults who are in for premeditated murder, when they, of all their cohorts, are the least likely to be premeditators who think about consequences. They had a gun, they threatened with the gun, then they hardly know how it happened that they shot the gun, because they were not thinking through to the consequences."

4. *Doing the right thing.* Students are taught to pick the response that is most likely to succeed and be effective in solving the problem and preventing violence.

Slaby's research reveals that most youngsters in middle school want to hang out with individuals who know how to solve problems nonviolently, although they may not be consciously aware of this fact. This means that the classroom teacher can teach these skills and ways of thinking. Some youngsters know them already, but even those students profit from more practice. But some youth are at high risk and need to be taught how to prevent violence. "When kids do learn these skills and challenge the superficial beliefs that support violence," Slaby says, "their behavior changes."

Picking Prevention Programs

Several researchers have called into question the effectiveness of some of the most popular anti-violence programs currently used by schools, charging that most schools are responding to the violence issue with "off-the-shelf" curriculum packages squeezed into the already-crowded curriculum. For example, Daniel Webster of the Injury Prevention Center at Johns Hopkins University found "no evidence" that three of the leading curriculum packages "produce long-term changes in violent behavior or risk of victimization." Webster concluded that the programs were a way for school officials and politicians to find "political cover" in the violence debate.

Renée Wilson-Brewer and her colleagues at the Education Development Center in Newton, Massachusetts, examined the claims of 51 programs and found that only half even *claimed* to be able to affect violent behavior.

The APA suggests intervention to counteract and deflect the forces that contribute to violent behavior. But the proliferation of new anti-violence programs requires parents, schools, and communities to make wise choices. The APA notes that many new programs have not been adequately tested or were not research-based in the first place. In short, the APA recommends that schools use only programs that share two basic characteristics:

• an understanding of developmental and sociocultural risk factors that lead to antisocial behavior; and

• the inclusion of theory-based intervention strategies with known effectiveness in changing behavior, tested program designs, and validated objective measurement techniques to assess outcomes.

The APA also recommends that programs "begin as early as possible," that they "address aggression as part of a constellation of antisocial behaviors in the child or youth," that their "multiple components reinforce each other across the child's everyday social contexts: family, school, peer groups, media, and community," and that they "take advantage of developmental windows of opportunity" when they are most needed or are most likely to make a difference.

The programs that the APA found to be most effective included home visitation components. School programs that "promote social and cognitive skills seem to have the greatest impact on attitudes about violent behavior among children and youth." Such skills include "perspective taking, alternative solution generation, self-esteem enhancement, peer negotiation skills, problem-solving training, and anger management." The APA encourages schools to differentiate between programs aimed at children already exhibiting violent behavior and those aimed at a more general audience.

A School Safety Plan

In the end, every school needs to adopt a broadly conceived and well-coordinated strategy to confront violence perpetrated against and by its students. The effort has barely begun in most communities and schools across the nation, even though the levels of concern are high.

A comprehensive plan to prevent school violence should start with issues of school safety and set concrete goals and objectives that will have immediate impact. Schools also need to be prepared for a crisis. The plan must decide how to train teachers, parents, and students in violence prevention. It should investigate curricula for violence prevention that match the real problems at the individual school. It must also find ways to make anti-violence a school expectation and theme. In addition, the plan should enlist the entire community in an effort to see that students can travel confidently to and from school through "safe" neighborhoods where businesspeople and parents constantly look out for their protection.

The school safety plan should chart ways to identify early those violent youths who need help, and it should specify how to arrange professional care for such children and teens. Perhaps the hardest part of a valid plan is finding ways to open up opportunities for these young people by making sure that every child and teen is in contact with adults who care about them, who mentor them, and who help them connect to their society through outside cultural or economic institutions. The plan should also find after-school alternatives for kids who have nowhere to go.

The Sixth Education Goal

In addition to protecting youth from assaults, each local school/community plan should stand as the first step toward fulfilling the sixth of our national goals for education, which calls for safe schools where learning is not disrupted. Students, teachers, principals, parents, police officers, and community members must be brought into the effort. And since the sixth goal is also a political goal—endorsed by two Presidents, by the Congress, and by all 50 state governors—schools should be given political support when they reach out for help. Moreover, if that support is not forthcoming, these politicians should be held responsible.

If the nation is ever to reach this all-important goal, which is a prerequisite for learning; if it is to spare its children from victimization, injury, psychic and physical pain, and potential death, even as they walk down a school hall or to and from the school; if it is to redeem the real promise of an American childhood, then it must, through its individual communities, launch some kind of campaign to prevent youth violence in order to make life safer for young people. Each person, each family, each community member, each teacher, and each student must take some of the responsibility for standing up to this devastating violence.

A truly effective campaign for the prevention of youth violence may require even more than the implementation of programs and campaigns. The radical reduction of youth violence probably will not happen until the entire society seeks and practices a more nonviolent way of resolving problems and emphasizes an ethic of valuing people. If we want children to learn nonviolent behavior, it seems reasonable that we need to exhibit nonviolent solutions to our social, economic, and even international problems. We must find ways to explain the consequences of violence more clearly to the nation's youth, as well as ways to enforce higher standards of personal behavior and responsibility. We need to set norms of nonviolent expectation and teach skills of social respect for ourselves and for our children.

"If we are going to have an impact on the schools, we're going to have to deal with all the other environmental issues, too," warns Donna Shalala, U.S. secretary of health and human services. Violence prevention "can't be seen simply as trying to make schools safe—because we have to try and make the streets safe as well." She is right. But intensifying the anti-violence message in schools is an important place to begin.

CRIME IN CYBERSPACE:
THE DIGITAL UNDERWORLD[7]

Billions of dollars in losses have already been discovered. Billions more have gone undetected. Trillions will be stolen, most without detection, by the emerging master criminal of the twenty-first century—the cyberspace offender.

Worst of all, *anyone* who is computer literate can become a cybercrook. He or she is everyman, everywoman, or even everychild. The crime itself will often be *virtual* in nature—sometimes recorded, more often not—occurring only in cyberspace, with the only record being fleeting electronic impulses.

But before discussing the infohighway crimes we can expect to see in the years ahead, let's look at the good news: The most-dreaded types of offenses—crimes such as murder, rape, assault, robbery, burglary, and vehicle theft—will be brought under control in the years ahead by a combination of technology and proactive community policing. Creation of the cashless society, for example, will eliminate most of the rewards for robbers and muggers, while computer-controlled smart houses and cars will thwart burglars and auto thieves. Implanted bodily function monitors and chemical drips (such as "sober-up" drugs and synthesized hormones) will keep most of the sexually and physically violent offenders under control.

More importantly, proactive policies—seeking out crime-breeding situations and taking steps to eliminate them before the crime occurs—may alleviate much of the burgeoning violence among young people. Tender, loving care demonstrated by informed parenting, universal health and day care, mentoring, and communal attention to children's welfare can prevent another generation of starved-for-attention juveniles from becoming criminals.

But cyberspace offenders—ranging in age from preteen to senior citizen—will have ample opportunities to violate citizens' rights for fun and profit, and stopping them will require much

[7]Article by Gene Stephens, professor in the College of Criminal Justice, University of South Carolina, from the September-October 1995 issue of *The Futurist* 29/5:24-8. Copyright © 1995 by World Future Society, Bethesda, Maryland. Reprinted with permission.

more effort. Currently, we have only primitive knowledge about these lawbreakers: Typically, they are seen only as nuisances or even admired as innovators or computer whizzes. But increasingly, the benign "hacker" is being replaced by the menacing "cracker"—an individual or member of a group intent on using cyberspace for illegal profit or terrorism.

Access to cyberspace has begun to expand geometrically, and technology is making the information superhighway even more friendly and affordable for millions of users. But foolproof protective systems can probably never be developed, although some high-tech entrepreneurs are certainly trying. Even if a totally secure system could ever be developed, it would likely disrupt the free flow of information—an unacceptable intrusion to most users. In fact, it is the ease of access that is driving this rapidly expanding field of crime.

What are the major cybercrimes being committed, how, and by whom? More importantly, where is cybercrime headed in the twenty-first century? Let's look at six cyberspace crime categories: communications, government, business, stalking, terrorism, and virtual.

Communications Crimes

Already, cellular theft and phone fraud have become major crimes. Low-tech thieves in airports and bus terminals use binoculars to steal calling-card access numbers as unsuspecting callers punch in their phone codes. Other thieves park vans beside busy interstate highways and use equipment obtained from shopping mall electronics stores to steal cellular phone access codes from the air. Within moments of these thefts, international calls are being made with the stolen numbers in what is becoming a multi-billion-dollar-a-year criminal industry.

Phone company employees, meanwhile, are also stealing and selling calling card numbers, resulting in more hundreds of millions of dollars in unauthorized calls. In 1994, an MCI engineer was charged with selling 60,000 calling card numbers for $3 to $5 each, resulting in more than $50 million in illegal long-distance charges. In another case, when a phone company tried to institute a call-forwarding program, crackers quickly defrauded the system of more money than the company stood to make in legal profits.

In the future, the opportunities for hacking and cracking will escalate, with telephones, computers, faxes, and televisions interconnected to provide instantaneous audiovisual communication and transmission of materials among individuals. The wide appeal of new multimedia communication systems will likely create such a huge volume of subscribers that the price will plummet and make access by all possible. But if billions of dollars of losses to thieves are compounded by billions more required to repair damages created by system terrorists, the cost might become prohibitive to all but the wealthy.

Cybercrimes Against the Government

In 1995, the U.S. Internal Revenue Service instituted stringent new regulations on electronic tax filing and returns. This move was to stop a rash of fraud that cost taxpayers millions in 1994: Returns that were processed quickly via this method turned out to be for tens of thousands of fictitious corporations and individuals. Similarly, in an attempt to stop food-stamp fraud, the government issued electronic debit cards to a trial population and plans to go nationwide with the system later in the decade. However, early reports show that many recipients are selling their benefits for cash—50¢ to 60¢ on the dollar—to merchants who then receive full payment.

Cyberpunks regularly break into government computer systems, usually out of curiosity and for the thrill of the challenge. They often intercept classified data and sometimes even interrupt and change systems. One U.S. Justice Department official reported that military computers are the most vulnerable, "even less secure than university computers." This official noted that, during Operation Desert Storm, hackers were able to track both actual and planned troop movements.

James V. Christy II, director of an Air Force unit of computer-crime investigators, set up a team of hackers to test the security of military computer systems. He reported that the hackers broke into Pentagon systems "within 15 seconds" and went on to break into over 200 Air Force systems with no one reporting or even recognizing the break-ins.

Ironically, computer hackers often beat the system using the very technology intended to stop them. For example, federal law-enforcement agencies use an Escrowed Encryption Standard to protect classified information and a chip-specific key to decrypt the system. Experienced hackers can easily discover the key and use it to obtain passwords, gaining full access to encrypted systems.

Newer, more-secure encryption systems for protecting government and international business transactions require storing the "keys" in "escrow" with a specific government agency—usually the U.S. Treasury Department. Hackers and civil libertarians find this security solution unacceptable because it impedes the free flow of information and puts almost all sensitive and important data in the hands of government officials. This is seen by many as being dangerous to individual freedoms and a major step in the direction of creating a class structure based on the "information rich" and "information poor."

As more government data is stored in computers, protection will become both more vital and more difficult. When the livelihood of an individual depends on data in government computers, the temptation to "adjust" that record to increase benefits and reduce charges will be great. Many will try to do the adjusting themselves; others will be willing customers for a burgeoning black market of professional crackers. For those who have little need for government benefits but would like to eliminate their tax liability, a highly destructive method would be to plant a computer virus in government computers to destroy large numbers of records. In this way, suspicion would not fall on an individual.

Targeting Business

Today, most banking is done by electronic impulse, surpassing checks and cash by a wide margin. In the near future, nearly all business transactions will be electronic. Thus, access to business computers equals access to money.

Recently, computer hacker John Lee, a founder of the infamous "Masters of Deception" hacker group, discussed his 10-year career, which began when he was 12 years old and included a one-year prison term in his late teens. Without admitting to any wrongdoing, Lee said that he could "commit a crime with five keystrokes" on the computer. He could: (1) change credit records and bank balances; (2) get free limousines, airplane flights, hotel rooms, and meals "without anyone being billed"; (3) change utility and rent rates; (4) distribute computer software programs free to all on the Internet; and (5) easily obtain insider trading information. Though prison was "no fun," Lee admitted that he would certainly be tempted to do it all again.

In a groundbreaking study published in *Criminal Justice Review* in the spring of 1994, Jerome E. Jackson of the California State University at Fresno reported the results of a study of a new group of criminals he called "fraud masters." These professional thieves obtain credit cards via fake applications, or by electronic theft, and pass them around among their peers internationally for profit. These young men and women want the "good life" after growing up in poverty. They are proud of their skills of deception and arrogant enough to feel they won't be caught. Indeed, none of those in the five-year case study were caught.

As seen in the $50-million-plus losses in the MCI case, a far greater threat to businesses than hackers are disgruntled and financially struggling employees. As internal theft from retail stores has always been many times greater in volume than theft from shoplifters, robbers, and burglars, theft by employees armed with inside information and computer access is and will continue to be a much larger problem than intrusion by hackers, crackers, and terrorists combined. By the turn of the century, 80% of Americans will process information as a major part of their employment, according to a United Way study.

In addition, the future portends new and brighter "for-profit" invasion of business computers. As one Justice Department official warns, "This technology in the hands of children today is technology that adults don't understand." The first generation of computer-literate citizens will reach adulthood shortly after the turn of the century and will surely open a new age in the annals of crime and crime-fighting.

Cyberstalking

One frightening type of cybercriminal emerging rapidly is the cyberstalker. Possibly the most disturbing of these criminals is the pedophile who surfs computer bulletin boards, filled with bright young boys and girls, in search of victims. He develops a cyberspace relationship and then seeks to meet the child in person to pursue his sexual intentions. Already recognized as a serious problem, cyberstalking has spawned the cybercop—a police officer assigned to computer bulletin boards in search of these pedophiles. Once a suspect is spotted, the cybercop plays the role of a naive youngster and makes himself or herself available for a meeting with the suspect in hopes of gaining evidence for an arrest.

Also surfing the network, in search of pedophiles, are computer pornography sellers who offer magazine-quality color photographs of young boys and girls in a variety of sexually suggestive or actual sexual acts. Such a ring was broken up in 1994 and was found to have clients in several countries, with the pictures themselves transmitted from Denmark.

Another type of stalker expected to be seen more in the future is the emotionally disturbed loner, seeking attention and companionship through cyberspace, and who often becomes obsessed with a bulletin board "friend." If this person obtains personal information about the cyberspace acquaintance, he or she sometimes seeks a close, often smothering relationship. If spurned, the stalker launches a campaign of cyberspace harassment, moving into real-space harassment if adequate information is obtained. Cyberspace vengeance can take many forms, from ruining credit records and charging multiple purchases to the victim to creating criminal records and sending letters to employers informing them of the "shady background" of the victim.

In the twenty-first century, with access to the information superhighway available to all and information from data banks networked into dossiers reserved for "official use only" (but easily accessible to hackers and crackers), stalking will not only increase but be facilitated by a new generation of portable computers. Organic nanocomputers may one day be implanted in the human brain, making possible a new crime: mindstalking. Unauthorized intrusion and seduction will reach directly into the victim's brain, making the stalker harder to evade and even more difficult to escape.

Remote Terrorism

In London a couple of years ago, terrorists placed deadly missiles in the back of a truck and remotely sent them flying toward the home of the British prime minister. The missiles exploded on the lawn without harm to the prime minister or the house, but they could have killed him and created an international crisis—clearly the intent of the bombers.

Today, terrorists have the capacity to detonate explosives in another country by means of computers and radio signals bounced off satellites. Because the emerging information superhighway is without borders, computer viruses and other information-destroying instruments can be hurled at business or government officials and facilities from anywhere on the globe.

In the future, information will be so crucial to success in business and personal life that being cut off from it will be like being held hostage or kidnapped. Terrorists who can cut communications off to an individual, group, community, or wider society will have the power and ability to spread fear and panic.

As with stalkers, terrorists will find new opportunities when computer implants in human brains become widely available. Borrowing a twentieth century technique from psychology—subliminal conditioning—terrorists might recruit unsuspecting accomplices via low-intensity audiovisual messages aimed directly at individuals with brain-implanted computers. Unsuspecting implantees might unconsciously begin to modify their attitudes in the direction sought by the terrorists, or worse, even begin to join in terrorist activities. Political terrorists, whose agenda often is to change the world to suit their beliefs, are the most likely candidates to embrace this new approach and other emerging technologies to gain direct access to the minds of the populace.

Virtual Crimes

Stock and bond fraud is already appearing in cyberspace—stocks and bonds that appear on the markets, are actively traded for a short time, and then disappear. The stocks and bonds are nonexistent; only the electronic impulses are real.

In a recent case, a trader was paid $9 million in commissions for what appeared to be some $100 million in sales of bonds. But investigators now feel that these bonds may never have changed hands at all, except in cyberspace. In the future, a virtual-reality expert could create a hologram in the form of a respected stockbroker or real estate broker, then advise clients in cyberspace to buy certain stocks, bonds, or real estate. Unsuspecting victims acting on the advice might later find that they had enlarged the coffers of the virtual-reality expert, while buying worthless or nonexistent properties.

This is just the tip of the iceberg in what might be tagged as "virtual crime"—offenses based on a reality that only exists in cyberspace. As virtual reality becomes increasingly sophisticated, it is the young adults in the first decade of the twenty-first century who—having grown up with virtual reality—will create the software and determine the legal and criminal uses of this technology. And with virtual reality potentially reaching directly into the brains of recipients via "organic" computers, the ability to separate cyberspace reality from truth outside cyberspace will be one of the greatest challenges of the twenty-first century.

Twenty-First Century Expectations

The outlook for curtailing cyberspace crime by technology or conventional law-enforcement methods is bleak. Most agencies do not have the personnel or the skills to cope with such offenses, and to date all high-tech approaches have been met by almost immediate turnabouts by hackers or crackers.

As individuals see and talk to each other over computers in the next few years, and as nanotechnology makes computers even more portable, new technology will emerge to protect data. But simplifying systems to make them more universally acceptable and accessible will also make them more vulnerable to intruders.

Control of access by optical patterns, DNA identification, voice spectrographs, encryption, and other methods may slow down hackers, but no method is foolproof or presents much of a challenge to today's most-talented cyberpunks. The trouble is that in the future many more users will have skills far beyond those of today's crackers—a process one expert termed "the democratization of computer crime."

Still, there is much to be gained by easy access to the information superhighway. The "cyberpunk imperatives," a code subscribed to many hackers, include: (1) information should be free so that the most capable can make the most of it; (2) the world will be better off if entrepreneurs can obtain any data necessary to provide needed or desired new products and services; and (3) decentralization of information protects us all from "Big Brother."

Cybercrime probably cannot be controlled by conventional methods. Technology is on the side of the cyberspace offender and motivation is high—it's fun, exciting, challenging, and profitable. The only real help is one that has not proven very success-ful in recent decades: conscience and personal values, the belief that theft, deception, and invasion of privacy are simply unac-ceptable.

Behavioral psychologists argue that all values are learned by a system of rewards and, to a lesser extent, punishment. Thus, if these values are necessary for survival, children should conscious-ly be conditioned to live by them. If all citizens—all computer us-ers—were taught these values and sought to live by them, cyberspace could become the wondrous and friendly place its cre-ators have envisioned.

Ironically, the greatest possible allies to be found in this search for values in cyberspace are the adolescent hackers of the 1980s, many of whom are the software programmers of the 1990s. In his book, *Secrets of a Super-Hacker,* a hacker named "Knightmare" says that "true hackers" love to break into systems and leave proof of their skills, but do not hurt individuals by steal-ing tangible goods or money, or destroying files or systems.

"Hacker ethics," "Knightmare" writes, include informing computer managers about problems with their security and offer-ing to teach and share knowledge about computer security when asked. Increasingly, government and business computer manag-ers are asking. Many of the Fortune 500 companies and numer-ous government agencies have hired hackers to test their systems and even design new security protocols for them.

Thus, hackers are helping to protect the information super-highway from crackers and terrorists. As one hacker says, "Hackers love computers and they want the Net safe."

II. CAUSES

EDITOR'S INTRODUCTION

There are many theories as to why people become criminals. Among the reasons most cited are poverty and unemployment. But even though the root causes of crime are officially considered to be material conditions, Patrick Fagan is not completely convinced. His speech, "The Real Root Cause of Violent Crime," delivered in Hillsdale, Michigan, reminds us that the Violent Crime Control and Law Enforcement Act of 1994 provides billions of dollars in new spending and adds fifteen new social programs to a system that has cost taxpayers $5 trillion since the mid-1960s. Fagan continues by explaining that, though welfare spending has increased 800 percent since the War on Poverty, the number of felonies per capita in the United States has also increased, to nearly three times the rate prior to 1960. The speaker blames family structure, rather than material want, for causing young people to enter a pattern leading ultimately to criminal activity. In "What to Do About Crime," James Q. Wilson believes that while there is a statistical relationship between poverty and crime, it is only a weak relationship, and that many increases in crime have occurred in times of national prosperity and well-being.

Some believe there are other factors besides a poor family structure or poverty that foster crime in America. According to articles by Julian Williams in *Discover* and Robert Wright in the *New Yorker*, genetics and biology can play a large role in determining who will and will not turn to crime. Both articles address the questions that arise, even without conclusive scientific data, from such studies. In 1992 a planned conference on "genetic factors in crime" had its federal funding pulled and was accused of "fostering racial prejudice," as Williams reports. Wright discusses similar instances of concern over the possible consequence of this very different approach to the study of crime and criminals.

THE REAL ROOT CAUSE OF VIOLENT CRIME[1]

The Breakdown of the Family

Social scientists, criminologists, and many other observers at long last are coming to recognize the connection between the breakdown of families and various social problems that have plagued American society. In the debate over welfare reform, for instance, it is now a widely accepted premise that children born into single-parent families are much more likely than children born into intact families to fall into poverty and welfare dependency.

While the link between the family and chronic welfare dependency is much better understood these days, there is another link—between the family and crime—that deserves more attention. Why? Because whole communities, particularly in urban areas, are being torn apart by crime. We desperately need to uncover the real root cause of criminal behavior and learn how criminals are formed if we are to fight this growing threat.

There is a wealth of evidence in the professional literature of criminology and sociology to suggest that the breakdown of family is the real root cause of crime in America. But the orthodox thinking in official Washington assumes that crime is caused by material conditions, such as poor employment opportunities and a shortage of adequately funded state and federal social programs.

The Violent Crime Control and Law Enforcement Act of 1994, supported by the Clinton administration and enacted last year, perfectly embodies official Washington's view of crime. It provides for billions of dollars in new spending, adding 15 new social programs on top of a welfare system that has cost taxpayers $5 trillion since the "War on Poverty" was declared in 1965. But there is no reason to suppose that increased spending and new programs will have any significant positive impact. Since 1965,

[1]Speech delivered by Patrick Fagan, Fitzgerald Fellow, Heritage Foundation at The Center for Constructive Alternatives Seminar, Hillsdale College, Michigan on February 5, 1995, from *Vital Speeches of the Day* 62/5:157-8. Copyright © 1995 by City News Publishing Co. Reprinted with permission.

welfare spending has increased 800 percent in real terms, while the number of major felonies per capita today is roughly three times the rate prior to 1960. As Republican Senator Phil Gramm rightly observes, "If social spending stopped crime, America would be the safest country in the world."

Still, federal bureaucrats and lawmakers persist in arguing that poverty is the primary cause of crime. In its simplest form, this contention is absurd; if it were true, there would have been more crime in the past, when more people were poorer. And, in poorer nations, the crime rates would be higher than in the United States. History defies the assumption that deteriorating economic circumstances breed crime and that improving conditions reduce it. America's crime rate actually rose during the long period of real economic growth in the early 20th century. As the Great Depression set in and incomes dropped, the crime rate also dropped. It rose again between 1965 and 1974 when incomes rose. Most recently, during the recession of 1982, there was a slight dip in crime, not an increase.

Official Washington also believes that race is the second most important cause of crime. The large disparity in crime rates between whites and blacks is often cited as proof. However, a closer look at the data shows that the real variable is not race but family structure and all that it implies in terms of commitment and love between adults and between adults and children. A major 1988 study of 11,000 individuals found that "the percentage of single-parent households with children between the ages of 12 and 20 is significantly associated with rates of violent crime and burglary." The same study makes it clear that the popular assumption that there is an association between race and crime is false. Illegitimacy, not race, is the key factor. It is the absence of marriage and the failure to form and maintain intact families that explains the incidence of crime among whites as well as blacks.

There is a strong, well-documented pattern of circumstances and social evolution in the life of a future violent criminal. The pattern may be summarized in five basic stages.

STAGE ONE: Parental neglect and abandonment of the child in early home life.

• When the future violent criminal is born his father has already abandoned the mother.

• If his parents are married, they are likely to divorce by the third year.

• He is raised in a neighborhood with a high concentration of single-parent families.

• He does not become securely attached to his mother during the critical early years of his life.

• His child care frequently changes.

• The adults in his life frequently quarrel and vent their frustrations physically.

• He, or a member of his family, may suffer one or more forms of abuse, including sexual abuse.

• There is much harshness in his home, and he is deprived of affection.

• He becomes hostile, anxious, and hyperactive. He is difficult to manage at age three and is frequently labeled as a "behavior problem."

• Lacking his father's presence and attention, he becomes increasingly aggressive.

STAGE TWO: The embryonic gang becomes a place for him to belong.

• His behavior continues to deteriorate at a rapid rate.

• He satisfies his needs by exploiting others.

• At age five or six, he hits his mother.

• In first grade, his aggressive behavior causes problems for other children.

• He is difficult for school officials to handle.

• He is socially rejected at school by "normal" children.

• He searches for and finds acceptance among similarly aggressive and hostile children.

• He and his friends are slower at school. They fail at verbal tasks that demand abstract thinking and at learning social and moral concepts.

• His reading scores trail behind the rest of his class.

• He has lessening interest in school, teachers, and in learning.

• By now, he and his friends have low educational and life expectations for themselves.

• These low expectations are reinforced by teachers and family members.

• Poor supervision at home continues.

• His father, or father substitute, is still absent.

• His life is now primarily characterized by his own aggressive behavior, his aggressive peers, and his hostile home life.

STAGE THREE: He joins a delinquent gang.

• At age 11, his bad habits and attitudes are well established.

• By age 15, he engages in criminal behavior (And the earlier he commits his first delinquent act, the longer he will be likely to lead a life of crime.)

• His companions are the main source of his personal identity and his sense of belonging.

• Life with his delinquent friends is hidden from adults.

• The number of delinquent acts increases in the year before he and his friends drop out of school.

• His delinquent girlfriends have poor relationships with their mothers, as well as with "normal" girls in school.

• Many of his peers use drugs.

• Many, especially the girls, run away from home or just drift away.

STAGE FOUR: He commits violent crime and the full-fledged criminal gang emerges.

• High violence grows in his community with the increase in the number of single-parent families.

• He purchases a gun, at first mainly for self-defense.

• He and his peers begin to use violence for exploitation.

• The violent young men in his delinquent peer group are arrested more than the non-violent criminals. But most of them do not get caught at all.

• Gradually, different friends specialize in different types of crime: violence or theft. Some are more versatile than others.

• The girls are involved in prostitution while he and the other boys are members of criminal gangs.

STAGE FIVE: A new child—and a new generation of criminals—is born.

• His 16-year-old girlfriend is pregnant. He has no thought of marrying her; among his peers this simply isn't done. They stay together for awhile until the shouting and hitting start. He leaves her and does not see the baby anymore.

• One or two of his criminal friends are real experts in their field.

• Only a few members of the group to which he now belongs—career criminals—are caught. They commit hundreds of crimes per year.

• Most of the crimes he and his friends commit are in their own neighborhood.

For the future violent criminal, each of these five stages is characterized by the absence of the love, affection, and dedication of his parents. The ordinary tasks of growing up are a series of perverse exercises, frustrating his needs, stunting his capacity for empathy as well as his ability to belong, and increasing the risk of his becoming a twisted young adult. This experience is in stark contrast to the investment of love and dedication by two parents normally needed to make compassionate, competent adults out of their children.

When you consider some of the alarming statistics that make headlines today, the future of our society appears bleak. In the mid-1980s, the chancellor of the New York City school system warned: "We are in a situation now where 12,000 of our 60,000 kindergartners have mothers who are still in their teenage years and where 40 percent of our students come from single-parent households." But today this crisis is not confined to New York City; it afflicts even small, rural communities. And, worse yet, the national illegitimacy rate is predicted to reach 50 percent within the next twelve to twenty years. As a result, violence in school is becoming worse. The Centers for Disease Control recently reported in one study that more than 4 percent of high school students surveyed had carried a firearm at least once to school. Many of them were, in fact, regular gun carriers.

The old injunction is clearly true: Violence begets violence. Violent families are producing violent youths, and violent youths are producing violent communities. The future violent criminal is likely to have witnessed numerous conflicts between his parents. He may have been physically or sexually abused. His parents, brothers, and sisters may also be criminals, and thus his family may have a disproportionate negative impact on the community. Moreover, British and American studies show that fewer than 5 percent of all criminals account for 50 percent of all criminal convictions.

Overall, there has been an extraordinary increase in community violence in most major American cities. Between 1989 and 1990, for example, the homicide rate in Boston increased by over 40 percent; in Denver, it rose by 29 percent; in Chicago, Dallas, and New Orleans, by more than 20 percent; in Los Angeles, by 16 percent; in New York, by 11 percent.

Government agencies are powerless to make men and women marry or stay married. They are powerless to guarantee parents will love and care for their children. They are powerless to persuade anyone to make and keep promises. In fact government agencies often do more harm than good by enforcing policies that undermine stable families and by misdiagnosing the real root cause of such social problems as violent crime.

But ordinary Americans are not powerless. They know full well how to fight crime effectively. They do not need to survey current social science literature to know that family life of affection, cohesion, and parental involvement prevents delinquency. They instinctively realize that paternal and maternal affection and the father's presence in the home are among the critical elements in raising well-balanced children. And they further acknowledge that parents should encourage the moral development of their children—moral development that is best accomplished within the context of religious belief and practice.

None of this is to say that fighting crime or rebuilding stable families and communities will be easy. But what is easy is deciding what we must do at the outset. We begin by affirming four simple principles: First, marriage is vital. Second, parents must love and nurture their children in spiritual as well as physical ways. Third, children must be taught how to relate to and empathize with others. And, finally, the backbone of strong neighborhoods and communities is friendship and cooperation among families.

These principles constitute the real root solution to the real root problem of violent crime. We should do everything in our power to apply them in our own lives and the life of the nation, not just for our sake, but for the sake of our children.

VIOLENCE, GENES, AND PREJUDICE[2]

As scientific debates go, the war of words over the genetic roots of violence has itself been marked by unusual violence. It has damaged careers, provoked comparisons with Nazi pogroms,

[2]Article by Juan Williams from *Discover* 15/11:93-102 N '94. Juan Williams/ © 1994 The Walt Disney Co. Reprinted with permission of Discover Magazine.

and prompted bitter talk of science being corrupted by political correctness. It has also sparked passionate statements about racists, Luddites, and monkey sex. This is the stuff of great fiction.

But it's true. And the arguments are only likely to get fiercer as violence in America continues to rise.

Let's leave aside for the moment the question of whether a convincing connection can yet be made between certain genes and violent behavior. Even without conclusive evidence that it can, heated questions are being raised. Will the government try to screen people to see if they have genes that incline them to violence? If people do have such a gene, can they be forced into medical therapy? What if tests are used selectively to screen minority children, on the grounds that a growing number of American prison inmates are black or Hispanic? "Research into genetic factors has tremendous impact, and it is likely to yield controversial findings that are highly susceptible to abuse and misunderstanding," says David Wasserman, who teaches philosophy of law, medicine, and social science at the University of Maryland's Institute of Philosophy and Public Policy.

Wasserman knows what he is talking about; he has already been burned by the debate. A 1992 conference he planned on "genetic factors in crime" had its federal funding yanked after it was denounced for fostering racial prejudice and promoting a "modern-day version of eugenics." Research presented at the conference, its more vehement opponents protested to the *New York Times*, "would inevitably target minority children in the inner city in the guise of preventing future crime."

Wasserman adamantly denies those charges. "Scientists were brought to this subject by legitimate curiosity," he says. "They did not wake up one day having been mugged and say, 'Let's see if there is a gene responsible for crime.' Scientists see themselves as increasing understanding of human behavior—though they may be naive about the implications of their research and the political agendas it might further."

Ironically, current efforts to assess what role biology and genetics might play in violent human behavior started out with the best of intentions, at least from the point of view of the people behind them.

One of those people was Louis Sullivan, the Bush administration's secretary of health and human services from 1989 to 1993.

Sullivan was appalled by the epidemic of violence he saw taking place in American cities. In 1992 more than 26,000 Americans were murdered, and 6 million violent crimes were committed, with young men and minorities falling victim most frequently. One in every 27 black men, compared with one in 205 white men, died violently; one in 117 black women met the same fate, as compared with one in 496 white women. And a disproportionate amount of the violence to blacks was being done by blacks, in poor, underserved urban neighborhoods. Black Americans, who constitute about 12 percent of the population, were arrested for 45 percent of the nation's violent crimes.

Sullivan, a black physician who is now president of Morehouse School of Medicine in Atlanta, wanted to try addressing violence as a public health issue. "The rationale for this was the high incidence of violence and homicide in young black people and particularly young black males," he explained last July in the first interview he has given on the controversy since leaving office. "The hope was that we could diagnose the likelihood of violence occurring and learn how we might intervene, in terms of counseling families and individuals."

To that end, Sullivan began organizing his department's research resources under the banner of the "Violence Initiative." "At the time we got into this," he says, "the predominant thought was to look at unemployment, poverty, use of illicit drugs—a whole range of factors that might contribute to the likelihood of violence. I wanted to bring together the various components that could help us address the question of violent behavior, primarily from the psychological and sociological point of view." Some of this research had biological aspects, of course, including studies that looked at people's brain chemistry and even their genes. But these studies, largely done at the National Institutes of Health (NIH), formed only a fraction of the initiative, accounting for .5 percent of its budget. They were hardly uppermost in Sullivan's mind—he saw the overriding problems as social—yet it was precisely these studies that came to haunt him.

Among them were some exploring the link between aggressive behavior and disturbances in levels of a chemical called serotonin. Gerald L. Brown, a psychiatrist who is clinical director of the National Institute on Alcohol Abuse and Alcoholism, explains that serotonin transmits nerve signals in the brain and is important in regulating sleep, sexual behavior, appetite, and impulsivity. In 1979 Brown was part of the team that first suggested an association between low levels of serotonin and out-of-control aggressive behavior in a group of U.S. military men. Serotonin depletion appears to have a disinhibiting effect, says Brown, and studies have repeatedly implicated it in explosive, destructive, impulsive behavior, including suicide. "A more familiar word might be *violent*," he adds, "but *violent* is not a scientific term; it's descriptive."

Many things can apparently influence serotonin production, though race isn't one of them. Serotonin levels are 20 to 30 percent lower in men than in women. They are high in newborns, low in adolescents, then rise again with age—a pattern that seems to fit with the stereotype of the impulsive teenager. A diet high in L-tryptophan, an amino acid needed to make serotonin, can boost levels of the neurotransmitter in animals. Some studies tentatively suggest that animals subjected to stressful environments make less serotonin, raising the possibility that the same might happen in humans living under the gun, whether on the battlefield or in poor, crime-ridden neighborhoods.

But there's a suspicion that genes, too, influence serotonin metabolism and behavior, making certain people more susceptible to impulsivity, especially under stress. So some researchers have begun to hunt for signs of gene defects or genetic variants associated with abnormal serotonin metabolism. Last year, for the first time, a mutation that apparently leads to serotonin disturbances was found in male members of a Dutch family with low IQ and a history of violence—though whether the defect is vanishingly rare or will turn up in other impulsive, aggressive people isn't yet known. Since then another study has turned up a genetic variant in violent, suicidal Finnish men. That's not to say that the case for linking genes to violence has by any means been proved—this research is still in its infancy. "What's more," points out Evan Balaban, a neurobiologist at the Neurosciences Institute in La Jolla, California, "serotonin is a neurotransmitter that affects many behaviors, not just aggression. So to specify that serotonin affects one type of behavior more than any other is very difficult." Nevertheless, some mental health specialists have already raised the possibility that doctors might one day use genetic markers to screen patients with behavioral disorders and treat serotonin abnormalities with drugs.

When Sullivan was formulating his ideas on the Violence Initiative, however, he gave only a passing nod to studies linking violent behavior to genes. "My focus was on situational factors," he recalls, with the tone of a man reconstructing how his car ended up in a ditch. "I was looking at drug use, absence of male role models, job loss, any factor other than genetic." But just as Sullivan's program was coming to life as the centerpiece of a Republican administration's expression of concern over violence in the ghetto, it was buried.

The killing blow was struck by a friend. One of the scientists Sullivan had consulted about the Violence Initiative was Frederick Goodwin, then director of the Alcohol, Drug Abuse, and Mental Health Administration. "Lou Sullivan had turned to me and said this epidemic of violence concerned him," recalls Goodwin, who, like Sullivan, has avoided interviews since the controversy left him feeling misunderstood and unfairly hounded by race baiters. "We had a 1992 national survey of young offenders," he says. "And we found that when we looked at youth offenses involving some form of violence, 80 percent of the offenses were committed by 7 percent of the population. It was an incredible concentration. So the first thing we looked for was correlation— an association between this 7 percent and some other factor. And I want to make clear there was no correlation between violence and race at all, when you took socioeconomic status out of it—in fact, black middle-class kids, we'd previously found, were less likely to abuse drugs than white middle-class kids and were more socially responsible. There *was*, however, a strong association of violence with low socioeconomic class. Nevertheless, there were a lot more people of low socioeconomic status who were *not* violent than who were violent, so class was not deterministic. There had to be something else influencing violent behavior."

In February 1992, Goodwin made some casual remarks at a meeting of the Mental Health Advisory Council, reflecting on violence as a public health concern. He drew an analogy between the behavior of male rhesus monkeys in the wild and violent young men in tough city neighborhoods. Although he did not specify young black men, some people in the audience clearly thought that's who he was referring to. "If you look, for example, at male monkeys, especially in the wild, roughly half of them survive to adulthood," Goodwin said. "The other half die by violence. That is the natural way of it for males, to knock each other off—and, in fact, there are some interesting evolutionary implications of that because the same hyperaggressive monkeys that kill each other are also hypersexual, so they copulate more."

Incensed, Delores Parron, associate director for special populations at the National Institute of Mental Health (NIMH), walked out on his talk. But Goodwin had no idea he was going down in flames. On the contrary, he went on to throw fat on the fire. "Now, one could save that some of the loss of social structure in this society, and particularly within the high-impact inner-city areas, has removed some of the civilizing evolutionary things that we have built up, and that maybe it isn't just careless use of the word when people call certain areas of certain cities 'jungles.' We may have gone back to what might be more natural, without all of the social controls that we have imposed upon ourselves as a civilization over thousands of years in our evolution." Along the way Goodwin mentioned that NIMH-funded scientists were also looking for biological and genetic factors underlying violence, though he concluded, "The loss of structure in society is probably why we are seeing the doubling incidence of violence among the young over the last twenty years."

Goodwin's remarks set off a political explosion. His talk of monkeys and jungles in the context of violence in the inner cities came too close to long-standing racist suggestions that blacks are genetic throwbacks, to be treated as animals, or as chattel to be enslaved. A headline in the *Washington Post* portrayed Goodwin as comparing VIOLENT YOUTHS IN INNER CITY TO AGGRESSIVE PRIMATES IN "JUNGLES." Sullivan reprimanded Goodwin, who publicly apologized for his "insensitivity" and the "inappropriateness" of his comments. In the spring of 1992 Goodwin was moved from overseeing the Alcohol, Drug Abuse, and Mental Health Administration to become head of the NIMH.

Today Goodwin is no longer a government official—he is director of the Center on Neuroscience, Behavior, and Society at George Washington University. But he is still pained by the hail of censure. "Basically, even mentioning genetic issues with blacks is difficult," he says. "People are understandably sensitive. They immediately start thinking 'eugenics' because of the terrible history of genetic slurring of blacks as inferior."

Goodwin kept a low profile after his public apology. Meanwhile his boss, Sullivan, was working hard to stay afloat in a sea of criticism. The genetics of behavior is always a touchy subject; the fact that Goodwin raised it in his remarks about the Violence Initiative, with its stated mission of curing inner-city ills, was unfortunate, to say the least. Rumors began to fly that the government was not so much interested in helping individuals with "genetic susceptibilities" as in looking for—and then exploiting—such susceptibilities in blacks. Sullivan, who had hoped to be a hero to a minority community bedeviled by violence, was now astounded to find himself painted as a villain. He was being pilloried as a black man who was collaborating with efforts to use science to deny black people their humanity—and his ordeal was not over. Less than three months after Goodwin's fateful comments, in May 1992, the fat was on the fire once again.

This time the blowup was prompted by the release of the program for David Wasserman's University of Maryland conference, entitled "Genetic Factors in Crime: Findings, Uses & Implications." "Researchers," the brochure began, "have already begun to study the genetic regulation of violent and impulsive behavior and to search for genetic markers associated with criminal conduct." It went on to point out that genetic research had gained impetus from "the apparent failure of environmental approaches to crime—deterrence, diversion, and rehabilitation—to affect the dramatic increases in crime" and that such research "holds out the prospect of identifying individuals who may be predisposed to certain kinds of criminal conduct, of isolating environmental features which trigger those predispositions, and of treating some predispositions with drugs and unintrusive therapies."

Sullivan, still bailing out a boat quickly sinking from sight, said his Violence Initiative had no connection with Wasserman's conference, even though the conference was funded by the NIH (an agency for which Sullivan, as secretary of health and human services, was ultimately responsible). But some critics immediately put the two together as evidence of a deepening conspiracy, with blacks and Hispanics as the likely targets. Children would be screened for genes that made them prone to crime, they warned, and given sedating drugs.

Among the more enraged critics was Samuel Yette, an author and former Howard University journalism professor. Yette, who is black, told the *Chronicle of Higher Education* that the conference would encourage the impression that blacks are born criminals. "It is an effort," he said, "to use public money for a genocidal effort against African Americans." White critics also invoked the specter of eugenics. In a letter to the *New York Times*, Norman Finkelstein of New York University pointed out that earlier this century eugenicists' theories linking criminality to genes—in this case to genes for "feeblemindedness" and "moral degeneracy"—had resulted in up to thirty states adopting forced-sterilization laws. "In 1927," wrote Finkelstein, "the Supreme Court upheld the constitutionality of sterilization, with Associate Justice Oliver Wendell Holmes declaring 'it is far better for all the world if instead of waiting to execute degenerate offspring for crime . . . society can prevent those who are manifestly unfit from continuing their kind.'" According to Finkelstein, more than 35,000 Americans were sterilized before World War II. "Germany," he noted, "did not pass such a law until 1933, and German eugenicists then stated they owed a great debt to the American precedent."

But the most visible—some would say publicity-seeking—critic of the project was Peter Breggin, a white psychiatrist and activist well known for opposing the use of drugs to treat psychiatric problems. In a story headlined PLOT TO SEDATE BLACK YOUTH, which ran in a small black newspaper in Washington, D.C., Breggin and fellow opponents implied that the gene studies slated for discussion at the conference formed the core of a massive social engineering scheme. A plan was afoot, they said, to identify potentially violent inner-city children on the basis of biological and genetic markers—paving the way for psychiatric intervention, including the widespread medication of black children. Breggin later repeated his views on a news show on Black Entertainment Television and led the attack against the conference through his organization, the Center for the Study of Psychiatry. In July 1992 the NIH, which had given Wasserman $78,400 to fund the conference the following October, withdrew its support.

But the fight was far from over. "This is political correctness," blasted Gary Stephenson, an official at the University of Maryland, where the conference was to be held. "Just having such a conference doesn't mean the university endorses racism or sexism," he told the *New York Times*. "The university provides an open forum for debate on controversial issues."

Writing in the *Chronicle of Higher Education*, Wasserman pointed out that the language of the controversial brochure was taken straight from the proposal he'd submitted requesting NIH funds for the meeting, which the NIH had rated "superb." In fact, the proposed meeting was praised for the diversity of its speakers, who ranged from those who believed genes play a role in violence to those worried about the legitimization of a link that was as yet unproved.

Showing a steely will, Wasserman did not shrink in the face of accusations of racism. Scientists doing this work, he said, were interested in understanding individual susceptibility to violence, not in exploiting alleged racial traits. "Several researchers at the conference would have dismissed the claim that one racial group is more predisposed genetically to crime than another as unsupported and inherently implausible," Wasserman wrote in his *Chronicle* article. "They would have argued that racial differences in crime rates were explained by powerful environmental factors." Though some researchers (not invited to the conference) claim that such racial differences are genetic, he continued, "their research is regarded as flimsy, even by strong proponents of individual genetic predispositions."

Wasserman concluded: "In sponsoring a debate on individual, but not racial, differences in genetic predisposition to criminal behavior, I believe that I have drawn a defensible line." In another publication, *Black Issues in Higher Education*, he added that the decision to cancel the conference was "not formed out of concern for the black community" but for political reasons. "This is an election year, remember, and the Bush people are very sensitive."

The op-ed tide began to run the other way. Arthur Caplan, director of the Center for Biomedical Ethics at the University of Minnesota, wrote in Baltimore's *Evening Sun*: "In plain English," NIH director Bernadine Healy "yanked the funds because some people told her the topic of the genetics of crime is politically incorrect." An editorial in the *Journal of NIH Research* accused health and human services officials of a "lack of political courage . . . at a time when violence and crime dominate American life." The editorial went on: "At the heart of the controversy is a deep-seated fear of discovering that human behaviors, even violent ones, have biological roots. . . . What would we do with such information? The canceled Maryland conference was to address issues such as this." Five months after the NIH pulled its support for the conference, its grant appeals board ruled 7–2 to reinstate it. . . .

And what of the Violence Initiative? Though the name itself was dropped as a political embarrassment, the research it embraced essentially continues. In 1992 the federal government spent $53.7 million on NIH-funded violence studies. This year a panel of scientists, ethicists, and attorneys recommended substantially increasing the current $58 million budget. "Violence," the panel wrote in its April [1994] report to Harold Varmus, present director of the NIH, "is one of the leading causes of death and disability in our Nation." Its consequences exact "an extraordinarily heavy toll on our Nation's youth and elderly, and . . . disproportionately affect minority populations."

Looking back on the furor, Sullivan expresses no anger but rather a battle-weary sadness. "The thing in the background that really contributed to suspicions was Tuskegee," he reflects, referring to "a horrendous, inappropriate study" that began in rural Alabama in the 1930s. The Tuskegee study was a travesty of American public-health research. For decades 400 black men with syphilis were given what amounted to sham treatment so doctors could track the disease's unchecked progress. The study, which was halted under protest in 1972, left a sour taste in the black community. "Some say that AIDS was a disease developed in the lab to harm black people," notes Sullivan. "There is that lingering fear that somehow the government is plotting against its citizens to do some evil thing, which is unfortunate. It has slowed things tremendously."

Who could disagree? Lots of people, and passionately.

There's good reason to be wary of the way genetic findings are applied to society, says Troy Duster, director of the Institute for the Study of Social Change at the University of California at Berkeley. Duster, who is black, points out that past attempts to link inherited traits to criminal behavior have never held up. Recently, though, molecular biology has revolutionized genetics. "We can screen an individual's genes at the molecular level to see who's at risk for devastating medical disorders like Tay-Sachs, sickle-cell anemia, and cystic fibrosis," says Duster. "And these breakthroughs have created an unjustified halo effect for geneticists trying to explain behavior." The success of medical genetics shouldn't dazzle us into being uncritical about the pitfalls of behavioral genetics, he points out. Unlike, say, Tay-Sachs, which can be blamed on a single aberrant gene, violent behavior is likely to be the result of a fantastically intricate web of interactions among many genes and varying environments.

In his book, *Backdoor to Eugenics*, Duster argues that there are dangers in the way the public debate about genetics tends to be framed. On the one hand there are "experts (geneticists, medical specialists, researchers, etc.)" and on the other hand there are "critics who have been portrayed as naysayers and know-nothings, Luddites who would put their heads in the sand or try to stop the machinery of progress." As a result, he says, the typical citizen will always go along with the experts, just as "good Germans" went along with Nazi policies because they couldn't believe their leaders would start "selective extermination" of Jews and the mentally ill. In a similar vein, Duster fears that if the public buys the idea of "susceptibility genes" for violence, doesn't think to question their predictive power, and doesn't look out for their potential for abuse, then these genes could be used as a rationalization for political oppression of blacks.

Breggin goes even further. "This so-called scientific focus on violence in America basically means a focus on African Americans," he states. "What people are frightened about is little black children who are seen as having the seeds of destruction in them. Researchers are not looking to see if George Bush and his ne'er-do-well sons have bad genes. White people are looking at the victims of racism and saying something is wrong with them. But as soon as you say something is scientific, people get fooled. The argument used to be that blacks were docile and hence biologically predisposed to slavery. Now, in a few generations, they're supposed to be genetically predisposed to rebellion. This is not science. Evolution can't possibly work that fast. This is the use of psychiatry and science in the interest of racist social policy."

In the summer of 1992 Breggin, who is Jewish, personally appealed to Wasserman, who is also Jewish, to understand the dangers of holding a conference exploring genetics and violence. As Breggin describes it, they met by accident in a Bethesda pizza parlor. Breggin asked Wasserman how he would feel about a conference on "Genetic Factors in Junk Bond Dealing" at a time of public concern over the misdeeds of Michael Milkin and Ivan Boesky, who also happen to be Jewish.

Wasserman now dismisses Breggin as a "zealot." He notes that Breggin was the first to raise the specter of government-condoned, wide-scale medication of minority children. "Peter Breggin has a lot of chutzpah," says Wasserman, referring to Breggin's jump from genetic research on individual susceptibility to the use of drugs in a whole group of kids. "He made the leap, then decried it as racist."

In the past year, taking heed of all the criticism, the NIH has set up panels to review and provide guidance for its research on aggressive and antisocial behavior. Breggin, though, wasn't invited to sit on them. That job has fallen to a growing number of minority academics who are not necessarily opposed to the research but who want to be sure they have some say about the direction of the inquiry and how its results are presented to the public.

"There are few black biomedical scientists doing research, let alone this kind of research," points out Willie Pearson, a black sociologist at Wake Forest University in Winston-Salem, North Carolina; like Duster, he serves as an NIH reviewer. "So the first question becomes: Just who is doing the research, and how do you deal with the findings? What policy do you impose—and who is in on that policy? You can't assume that scientists are going to be objective. Science is not above being socialized, and people design research to fit their own paradigm. So I'm supportive of continuing gene research as long as it's reviewed by a more balanced group."

The second question that concerns Pearson is "whether this science is a rationalization for maintaining the status quo. Is it a legitimization for high arrest rates in black people? We don't need science that looks at America and says blacks and Hispanics have a high rate of homicide, so something must be biologically wrong with blacks and Hispanics."

That's a question that also concerns Richard Moran, a criminologist at Mount Holyoke College in South Hadley, Massachusetts. The idea that violent and criminal people are biologically flawed has a long history, he says. It extends back to Aristotle, "who believed that people came to look like particular animals and had that animal's traits—so sneaky people looked like weasels." In the late 1800s, inspired by Darwin, Italian physician Cesare Lombroso began measuring the heads, ears, feet, and jaws of convicts in an attempt to show that criminals were evolutionarily closer to animals than other humans. And at the turn of the century English physician Charles Goring—on the basis of his own measurements of convicts and university students—concluded that "in every class and occupation of life it is feeble mind and the inferior forms of physique which tend to be selected for a criminal career."

Moran thinks current research exploring genes and violence demonstrates the resilience of our fascination for studying criminals as a distinct biological subspecies. "The definition of the criminal offender has changed from someone who has done bad (morally guilty conduct) to someone who is bad or defective," he wrote in a set of essays called *Deviance and Medicalization*. His sentiment is shared by Jerry Miller, a leading criminologist who runs the National Center on Institutions and Alternatives in Alexandria, Virginia. "We have given up looking to social and environmental causes; that is passé," claims Miller. "And we have given up trying social and environmental solutions; we have said rehabilitation does not work. So what's left? Flawed people—and many of those people in jail are black." Miller fears that conservatives are looking for a reason to ignore social issues so they can launch a war against a "dehumanized and demonized 'enemy,' who too often these days turns out to have a black face."

Are there any voices of consensus amid this cacophony?

Diana Fishbein, a criminologist at the University of Baltimore, is all too familiar with the fear of urban crime. But she is also, as she puts it, "an integrationist. I believe very much in an interaction between the environment and genetic susceptibilities. That is to say, nobody is predestined to be violent. Nobody is predestined to be a criminal. But given a certain environment and a certain genetic predisposition, then the risk of violence can increase."

Fishbein's conclusion leads her to support social programs that cut down on stressful environments by providing for good schools, classes that teach parenting skills with the goal of reducing child abuse and neglect, and more social and employment programs. "Most people in our cities are not antisocial at all," says Fishbein. "But the inner cities are so adverse, in terms of poverty, unemployment, and hopelessness, that you're going to see more expressions of genetic disadvantages than you would in other environments."

It's a view that Goodwin could probably agree with, even though he would put it rather differently. "Anybody who says human behavior has nothing to do with biology is ignorant, and anyone who says human behavior is determined by biology is ignorant as well," says the man who lit the fuse that ignited this debate.

Can the debate—already the cause of so much anguish and anger, and by no means over—be worth it? With an issue as complex as this, a variety of voices and careful cross scrutiny might be the healthiest possible response.

Gerald Brown, who continues to study aggression at NIH, long ago reached that conclusion. "I'm a citizen and a scientist," he says. "I have no training in politics or social policy. I think we scientists should do our jobs well, under the scrutiny of scientific and ethical bodies. But I don't think we should be the ones to talk about social policy." He believes others should speak to that. Indeed, if there's one point on which many people can agree, it is this: genetic research on violence has to be seen in the context of a society desperately seeking solutions to violent crime—and perhaps all too ready to leap at simplistic explanations. In the circumstances, the price of apathy and silence might be even more painful than noise.

THE BIOLOGY OF VIOLENCE[3]

Frederick K. Goodwin has learned a lot during a lifetime of studying human behavior, but no lesson is more memorable than the one driven home to him over the past three years: becoming known as someone who compares inner-city teen-agers to monkeys is not a ticket to smooth sailing in American public life. As of early 1992, Goodwin's career had followed a steady upward course. He had been the first scientist to demonstrate clinically the antidepressant effects of lithium, and had become known as a leading, if not the leading, expert on manic-depressive illness. He had risen to become head of the Alcohol, Drug Abuse and

[3]Article by Robert Wright from *The New Yorker* 71/3:68-77 Mr 13 '95. Copyright © by *The New Yorker*. Reprinted with permission.

Mental Health Administration, the top position for a psychiatrist in the federal government, and was poised to be the point man in a policy that the Bush Administration was proudly unveiling: the Federal Violence Initiative. The idea was to treat violence as a public-health problem—to identify violently inclined youth and provide therapy early, before they had killed. The initiative had the strong support of the Secretary of Health and Human Services, Louis Sullivan, and Goodwin planned to make it his organization's main focus.

Then, in early 1992, while discussing the initiative before the National Mental Health Advisory Council, Goodwin made his fateful remarks. Speaking impromptu—and after a wholly sleepless night, he later said—he got off onto an extended riff about monkeys. In some monkey populations, he said, males kill other males and then, with the competition thus muted, proceed to copulate prolifically with females. These "hyperaggressive" males, he said, seem to be also "hypersexual." By a train of logic that was not entirely clear, he then arrived at the suggestion that "maybe it isn't just a careless use of the word when people call certain areas of certain cities jungles." Goodwin elaborated a bit on his obscure transition from monkeys to underclass males, but no matter, these few fragments are what came to form the standard paraphrase of his remarks. As the Los Angeles *Times* put it, Goodwin "made comparisons between inner-city youths and violent, oversexed monkeys who live in the wild."

As if a few seemingly racist quotes weren't enough of a public-relations bonanza for opponents of the Violence Initiative, Goodwin also injected what some took to be Hitlerian overtones. He talked about "genetic factors" inclining human beings toward violence, and suggested that one way to spot especially troublesome kids might be to look for "biological markers" of violent disposition. Within months, the Violence Initiative was abandoned, amid charges of racism. And Goodwin, facing the same charges, was reassigned to head the National Institute of Mental Health—not a huge demotion, but a conspicuous slap on the wrist. Finally, last year, he left that job for a position in academe after intermittent coolness from the Clinton Administration. Though no Clinton official ever told him he was a political liability, Goodwin found himself no longer invited to meetings he had once attended—meetings on violence, for example.

Goodwin is a victim of a vestigial feature of the American liberal mind: its undiscerning fear of the words "genetic" and "biological," and its wholesale hostility to Darwinian explanations of behavior. It turns out, believe it or not, that comparing violent inner-city males to monkeys isn't necessarily racist, or even necessarily right wing. On the contrary, a truly state-of-the-art comprehension of the comparison yields what is in many ways an archetypally liberal view of the "root causes" of urban violence. This comprehension comes via a young, hybrid academic discipline known as evolutionary psychology. Goodwin himself actually has little familiarity with the field, and doesn't realize how far to the left one can be dragged by a modern Darwinian view of the human mind. But he's closer to realizing it than the people whose outrage has altered his career.

As it happens, the nominally dead Federal Violence Initiative isn't really dead. Indeed, one of the few things Goodwin and his critics agree on is that its "life" and "death" have always been largely a question of labelling. Goodwin, who recently broke a thirty-month silence on the controversy, makes the point while dismissing the sinister aims attributed to the program. "They've made it sound like a cohesive new program that had some uniform direction to it and was directed by one person—namely, me," he told me. "The word 'initiative,' in bureaucratese, is simply a way of pulling stuff together to argue for budgets. In effect, that's what this was—a budget-formulation document, at Sullivan's request." Goodwin's critics look at the other side of the coin: just as the bulk of the Violence Initiative predated the name itself, the bulk of it survived the name's deletion. Thus the war against the violence initiative—lower case—must go on.

The person who was most responsible for turning Goodwin's monkey remarks into a life-changing and policy-influencing event is a psychiatrist named Peter Breggin, the founder and executive director of the Center for the Study of Psychiatry, in Bethesda, Maryland, just outside Washington. The center doubles as Breggin's home, and the center's research director, Ginger Ross Breggin, doubles as Breggin's wife. (Goodwin says of Peter Breggin, in reference to the center's lack of distinct physical existence, "People who don't know any better think he's a legitimate person.") Both Breggins take some credit for Goodwin's recent departure from government. "We've been all over the man for three years," Ginger Breggin observes.

Goodwin and Peter Breggin interned together at SUNY Upstate Medical Center in the 1960s. Both took a course taught by
Thomas Szasz, the author of "The Myth of Mental Illness," which
held that much of psychiatry is merely an oppressive tool by
which the powers that be label inconvenient behavior "deviant."
Szasz had formed his world view back when the most common
form of oppression was locking people up, and Breggin, since
founding his center, in 1971, has carried this view into the age
of psychopharmacology. He fought lithium, Goodwin's initial
claim to fame. He fought the monoamine-oxidase inhibitors, a
somewhat crude generation of antidepressants, and now he fights
a younger, less crude generation of them. "Talking Back to
Prozac," written in collaboration with his wife and published last
June, is among the anti-psychopharmacology books he has recently churned out. So is "The War Against Children," published
in which the Breggins attack Goodwin, the Violence Initiative,
and also the drug Ritalin. In Breggin's view, giving Ritalin to
"hyperactive" children is a way of regimenting spirited kids rather than according them the attention they need—just as giving
"anti-aggression" drugs to inner-city kids would be an excuse for
continued neglect. And Breggin is convinced that such drugs will
be used in precisely this fashion if the Goodwins of the world get
their way. This is the hidden agenda of the Violence Initiative,
he says. And Goodwin concedes that pharmacological therapy
was a likely outcome of the initiative.

Breggin's all-embracing opposition to psychopharmacology
has earned him a reputation among psychiatrists as a
"flat-earther." Some, indeed, go further in their disparagement,
and Breggin is aware of this. "I am not a kook," he will tell a reporter whether or not the reporter has asked. People try to dis-
credit him, Breggin says, because he is a threat to their
interests—to the money made by drug companies, which insidiously bias research toward chemical therapy, and to the power of
Goodwin and other "biological psychiatrists," who earn their status by "medicalizing" everything they see. "How is it that some
spiritually passionate people become labeled schizophrenic and
find themselves being treated as mental patients?" he asks in a
1991 book, "Toxic Psychiatry."

Breggin says he is struck by the parallels between the Violence Initiative and Nazi Germany: "the medicalization of social
issues, the declaration that the victim of oppression, in this case

the Jew, is in fact a genetically and biologically defective person, the mobilization of the state for eugenic purposes and biological purposes, the heavy use of psychiatry in the development of social-control programs." This is the sort of view that encouraged some members of the Congressional Black Caucus to demand that Goodwin be disciplined; it also helped get Breggin on Black Entertainment Television, and led to such headlines in black newspapers as "PLOT TO SEDATE BLACK YOUTH."

Breggin's scenario, the question of its truth aside, did have the rhetorical virtue of simple narrative form. ("He made a nice story of it," Goodwin says, in a tone not wholly devoid of admiration.) There has lately been much interest in, and much federally funded research into, the role that the neurotransmitter serotonin plays in violence. On average, people with low serotonin levels are more inclined toward impulsive violence than people with normal levels. Since Goodwin was a co-author of the first paper noting the correlation between serotonin and violence, he would seem to have a natural interest in this issue. And, since the "serotonin-reuptake inhibitors," such as Eli Lilly's Prozac, raise serotonin levels, there would seem to exist a large financial incentive to identify low serotonin as the source of urban ills. Hence, from Breggin's vantage point it all fell into place—a confluence of corporate and personal interests that helped make serotonin the most talked-about biochemical in federal violence research. But, Breggin says, we mustn't lose sight of its larger significance: serotonin is "just a code word for biological approaches."

It was in the late seventies that Goodwin and several colleagues stumbled on the connection between serotonin and violence, while studying servicemen who were being observed for possible psychiatric discharge. Since then, low serotonin has been found in other violent populations, such as children who torture animals, children who are unusually hostile toward their mothers, and people who score high for aggression on standardized tests. Lowering people's serotonin levels in a laboratory setting made them more inclined to give a person electrical shocks (or, at least, what experimenters deceived them into thinking were electrical shocks).

It isn't clear whether serotonin influences aggression per se or simply impulse control, since low serotonin correlates also with impulsive arson and with attempted suicide. But serotonin level does seem to be a rough predictor of misbehavior—a biological marker. In a study of twenty-nine children with "disruptive behavior disorders," serotonin level helped predict future aggression. And in a National Institutes of Health study of fifty-eight violent offenders and impulsive arsonists serotonin level, together with another biochemical index, predicted with eighty-four-percent accuracy whether they would commit crimes after leaving prison.

It doesn't take an overactive imagination to envision parole boards screening prisoners for biological markers before deciding their fate—just as Goodwin had suggested that using biological markers might help determine which children need antiviolence therapy. These are the kinds of scenarios that make Breggin worry about a world in which the government labels some people genetically deficient and treats them accordingly. In reply, Goodwin stresses that a "biological" marker needn't be a "genetic" one. Though NIH studies suggest that some people's genes are conducive to low serotonin, environmental influences can also lower serotonin, and federal researchers are studying these. Thus a "biological" marker may be an "environmental" marker, not a "genetic" one. To this Breggin replies, "It's not what they believe, it's not in a million years what they really believe." This attempt to cast biological research as research into environment "shows their desperation, because this was never their argument until they got attacked," he says. "It's a political move."

In truth, federal researchers, including Goodwin, were looking into "environmental influences" on biochemistry well before being attacked by Breggin. Still, they do often employ a narrower notion of the term's meaning than Breggin would like. When Goodwin talks about such influences, he doesn't dwell on the sort of social forces that interest Breggin, such as poverty and bad schools. He says, for example, that he has looked into "data on head injuries, victims of abuse, poor prenatal nutrition, higher levels of lead," and so on.

In other words, he is inclined to view violence as an illness, whether it is the product of aberrant genes or of pathological—deeply unnatural—circumstances, or both. This is not surprising, given his line of work: he is a psychiatrist, a doctor; his job is to cure people, and people without pathologies don't need curing. "Once I learned that seventy-nine percent of repeated violent offenses were by seven percent of youth, it began to look to me like a clinical population, a population that had something wrong with it that resulted in this behavior," he says. Other federal researchers on violence tend to take the same approach. After all, most of them work at one of the National Institutes of Health, whether the National Institute of Mental Health, the National Institute on Alcohol Abuse and Alcoholism, or some other affiliate. For the Violence Initiative to be successful in the pragmatic aims that Goodwin acknowledges—as a way "to argue for budgets" for the Department of Health and Human Services—it pretty much had to define violence as a pathology, characteristic of inner-city kids who have something "wrong" with them.

Breggin would rather depict violence as the not very surprising reaction of normal people to oppressive circumstances. A big problem with biological views of behavior generally, he says, is that they so often bolster the medical notions of "deviance" and "pathology"—and thus divert attention from the need to change social conditions.

But "biological" views don't have to be "medical" views. This is where the field of evolutionary psychology enters the picture, and modern Darwinian thought begins to diverge from Goodwin's sketchier and more dated ideas about human evolution. Evolutionary psychologists share Goodwin's conviction that genes, neurotransmitters such as serotonin, and biology more generally are a valid route to explaining human behavior; and they share his belief in the relevance of studying nonhuman primates. Yet they are much more open than he is to the Bregginesque view that inner-city violence is a "natural" reaction to a particular social environment.

To most NIH researchers, evolutionary psychology is terra incognita. Goodwin, for one, professes only vague awareness of the field. But the field offers something that should intrigue him: a theory about what serotonin is, in the deepest sense—why natural selection designed it to do the things it does. This theory would explain, for example, the effect that Prozac has on people. More to the point, this theory would explain the link that Goodwin himself discovered between low serotonin and violence.

The two acknowledged experts on human violence within evolutionary psychology are Martin Daly and Margo Wilson, of McMaster University, in Ontario. Their 1988 book, *Homicide,* barely known outside Darwinian-social-science circles, is considered a classic within them. Listening to Margo Wilson talk about urban crime is like entering a time warp and finding yourself chatting with Huey Newton or Jane Fonda in 1969. "First of all, what's a crime?" she asks. It all depends on "who are the rule-makers, who's in power. We call it theft when somebody comes into your house and steals something, but we don't call it theft when we get ripped off by political agendas or big-business practices." And as for gang violence: "It's a coalition of males who are mutually supporting each other to serve their interests against some other coalition. How is that different from some international war?"

To hear this sort of flaming liberal rhetoric from a confirmed Darwinian should surprise not just Peter Breggin but anyone familiar with intellectual history. For much of this century, many people who took a Darwinian view of human behavior embraced the notorious ideology of social Darwinism. They emphatically did not view social deviance as some arbitrary and self-serving designation made by the ruling class; more likely, crime was a sign of "unfitness," of an innate inability to thrive legitimately. The "unfit" were best left to languish in jail, where they could not reproduce. And "unfit" would-be immigrants—those from, say, Eastern Europe, who were congenitally ill equipped to enrich American society—were best kept out of the country.

What permits Margo Wilson to sound a quite different theme is two distinguishing features of evolutionary psychology. First, evolutionary psychologists are not much interested in genetic differences, whether among individuals or among groups. The object of study is, rather, "species-typical mental adaptations"—also known as "human nature." A basic tenet of evolutionary psychologists is that there *is* such a thing as human nature—that people everywhere have fundamentally the same minds.

A second tenet of evolutionary psychologists is respect for the power of environment. The human mind, they say, has been designed to adjust to social circumstances. The vital difference between this and earlier forms of environmental determinism is the word "designed." Evolutionary psychologists believe that the developmental programs that convert social experience into personality were created by natural selection, which is to say that those programs lie in our genes. Thus, to think clearly about the influence of environment we must think about what sorts of influences would have been favored by natural selection.

If, for example, early social rejection makes people enduringly insecure, then we should ask whether this pattern of development might have had a genetic payoff during evolution. Maybe people who faced such rejection saw their chances of survival and reproduction plummet unless they became more socially vigilant—neurotically attentive to nourishing their social ties. Thus genes that responded to rejection by instilling this neurotic vigilance, this insecurity, would have flourished. And eventually those genes could have spread through the species, becoming part of human nature.

These two themes—universal human nature and the power of environment—are related. It is belief in the power of environment—of family milieu, cultural milieu, social happenstance—that allows evolutionary psychologists to see great variation in human behavior, from person to person or from group to group, without reflexively concluding that the explanation lies in genetic variation. The explanation lies in the genes, to be sure. Where else could a program for psychological development ultimately reside? But it doesn't necessarily lie in differences among different people's genes.

This is the perspective that Martin Daly and Margo Wilson bring to the subject of violence. They think about genes in order to understand the role of environment. And one result of this outlook is agreement with Peter Breggin that inner-city violence shouldn't be labelled a "pathology." In a paper published last year Daly and Wilson wrote, "Violence is abhorrent. . . . Violence is so aversive that merely witnessing an instance can be literally sickening. . . . " There is thus "but a short leap to the metaphorical characterization of violence itself as a sort of 'sickness' or 'dysfunction.'" But, they insisted, this leap is ill advised. Violence is eminently functional—something that people are designed to do.

Especially men. From an evolutionary point of view, the leading cause of violence is maleness. "Men have evolved the morphological, physiological and psychological means to be effective users of violence," Daly and Wilson wrote. The reason, according to modern evolutionary thought, is simple. Because a female can reproduce only once a year, whereas a male can reproduce many times a year, females are the scarcer sexual resource. During evolution, males have competed over this resource, with the winners impregnating more than their share of women and the losers impregnating few or none. As always with natural selection, we're left with the genes of the winners—in this case, genes inclining males toward fierce combat. One reflection of this history is that men are larger and stronger than women. Such "sexual dimorphism" is seen in many species, and biologists consider it a rough index of the intensity of male sexual competition.

To say that during evolution men have fought over women isn't to say that they've always fought directly over women, with the winner of a bout walking over and claiming his nubile trophy. Rather, human beings are somewhat like our nearest relatives, the chimpanzees: males compete for status, and status brings access to females. Hence skills conducive to successful status competition would have a "selective advantage"—would be favored by natural selection. As Daly and Wilson have put it, "if status has persistently contributed to reproductive success, and a capacity for controlled violence has regularly contributed to status, then the selective advantage of violent skills cannot be gainsaid."

It's easy to find anecdotal evidence that status has indeed tended to boost the reproductive success of males. (It was Henry Kissinger who said that power is an aphrodisiac, and Representative Pat Schroeder who observed that a middle-aged congresswoman doesn't exert the same animal magnetism on the opposite sex that a middle-aged congressman does.) But more telling is evidence drawn from hunter-gatherer societies, the closest thing to real-life examples of the pre-agrarian social context for which the human mind was designed. Among the Ache of Paraguay, high-status men have more extramarital affairs and more illegitimate children than low-status men. Among the Aka Pygmies of central Africa, an informal leader known as a *kombeti* gets more wives and offspring than the average Aka. And so on. The Aka, the Ache, and Henry Kissinger all demonstrate that violence against other men is hardly the only means by which male status is sought. Being a good hunter is a primary route to status among the Ache, and being a wily social manipulator helps in all societies (even, it turns out, in chimp societies, where males climb the status ladder by forging "political" coalitions). Still, in all human societies questions of relative male status are sometimes settled through fighting. This form of settlement is, of course, more prevalent in some arenas than others—more in a bikers' bar than in the Russian Tea Room, more in the inner city than on the Upper East Side. But, as Daly and Wilson note, one theme holds true everywhere:

men compete for status through the means locally available. If men in the Russian Tea Room don't assault one another, that's because assault isn't the route to status in the Russian Tea Room.

According to Daly and Wilson, a failure to see the importance of such circumstances is what leads well-heeled people to express patronizing shock that "trivial" arguments in barrooms and ghettos escalate to murder. In *Homicide* they wrote, "An implicit contrast is drawn between the foolishness of violent men and the more rational motives that move sensible people like ourselves. The combatants are in effect denigrated as creatures of some lower order of mental functioning, evidently governed by immediate stimuli rather than by foresightful contemplation." In truth, Daly and Wilson say, such combatants are typical of our species, as it has been observed around the world: "In most social milieus, a man's reputation depends in part upon the maintenance of a credible threat of violence." This fact is "obscured in modern mass society because the state has assumed a monopoly on the legitimate use of force. But wherever that monopoly is relaxed— whether in an entire society or in a neglected underclass—then the utility of that credible threat becomes apparent." In such an environment, "a seemingly minor affront is not merely a 'stimulus' to action, isolated in time and space. It must be understood within a larger social context of reputations, face, relative social status, and enduring relationships. Men are known by their fellows as . . . people whose word means action and people who are full of hot air."

That a basic purpose of violence is display—to convince peers that you will defend your status—helps explain an otherwise puzzling fact. As Daly and Wilson note, when men kill men whom they know, there is usually an audience. This doesn't seem to make sense—why murder someone in the presence of witnesses?—except in terms of evolutionary psychology. Violence is in large part a performance.

Thus the dismay often inspired by reports that a black teenager killed because he had been "dissed" is naïve. Nothing was more vital to the reproductive success of our male ancestors than respect, so there is nothing that the male mind will more feverishly seek to neutralize than disrespect. All men spend much of their lives doing exactly this; most are just lucky enough to live in a place where guns won't help them do it. These days, well-educated men do their status maintenance the way Goodwin and

Breggin do it, by verbally defending their honor and verbally assailing the honor of their enemies. But back when duelling was in vogue even the most polished of men might occasionally try to kill one another.

This view from evolutionary psychology in some ways jibes with a rarely quoted point that Goodwin made during his rambling remarks on monkeys: that inner-city violence may be caused by a "loss of structure in society"; in an environment where violence is deemed legitimate, the male inclination for violence may reassert itself. Of monkeys, Goodwin had said, "that is the natural way of it for males, to knock each other off," and the implicit comparison was supposed to be with all human males, not just black ones; his point was that many black males now live in neighborhoods where social restraints have dissolved. This is the sense in which Goodwin says he meant to compare the inner cities to jungles, and the transcript of his remarks bears him out. His poor choice of imagery still haunts him. "If I had said that in the Wild West, where there was no structure, there was a hell of a lot of violence, no one would have noticed."

There is a crucial difference between this emphasis on social milieu as rendered by Goodwin and as rendered by evolutionary psychologists; namely, they don't abandon it when they start thinking about the interface between biology and environment. Whereas pondering this interface steers Goodwin's thoughts toward "pathology"—the biological effects of malnutrition, or brain damage due to child abuse—evolutionary psychologists try to figure out how normal, everyday experience affects the biochemistry of violence.

Consider serotonin. In particular, consider an extensive study of serotonin in monkeys done by Michael McGuire, an evolutionary psychologist, and his colleagues at U.C.L.A. Vervet monkeys have a clear male social hierarchy: low-status males defer to high-status males over access to limited resources, including females. McGuire found that the highest-ranking monkeys in the male social hierarchy have the highest serotonin levels. What's more, the lower-ranking males tend to be more impulsively violent. Other studies have linked low serotonin to violence in monkeys even more directly.

At first glance, such findings might appear to be what Peter Breggin, and many liberals, would consider their worst nightmare. If this biochemical analogy between monkeys and human beings is indeed valid, the lesson would seem to be this: some individuals are born to be society's leaders, some are born to be its hoodlums; the chairman of I.B.M. was born with high serotonin, the urban gang member was born with low serotonin. And what if it turns out that blacks on average have less serotonin than whites do?

There certainly is evidence that some sort of analogy between the social lives of monkeys and human beings is in order. McGuire has found that officers of college fraternities have higher serotonin levels than the average frat-house resident, and that college athletes perceived as team leaders have higher levels than their average teammate. But grasping the import of the analogy requires delving into the details of McGuire's monkey research.

When McGuire examines a dominant male monkey before he becomes a dominant—before he climbs the social hierarchy by winning some key fights with other males—serotonin level is often unexceptional. It rises during his ascent, apparently in response to sometimes inconspicuous social cues. Indeed, his serotonin may begin to creep upward before he physically challenges any higher-ranking males; the initial rise may be caused by favorable attention from females (who play a larger role in shaping the male social hierarchy than was once appreciated). When, on the other hand, a dominant male suffers a loss of status, his serotonin level drops.

What's going on here? There is no way to look inside a monkey's mind and see how serotonin makes him feel. But there is evidence that in human beings high serotonin levels bring high self-esteem. Raising self-esteem is one effect of Prozac and other serotonin boosters, such as Zoloft. And, indeed, high-ranking monkeys—or, to take a species more closely related to us, high-ranking chimpanzees—tend to behave the way people with high self-esteem behave: with calm self-assurance; assertively, yes, but seldom violently. (This subtle distinction, as Peter Kramer notes in "Listening to Prozac," is also seen in human beings. Prozac may make them more socially assertive, but less irritable, less prone to spontaneous outbursts.) To be sure, an alpha-male chimp may periodically exhibit aggression—or, really, a kind of ritual mock-aggression—to remind everyone that he's the boss, but most alphas tend not to be as fidgety and perturbable as some lower-ranking apes, except when leadership is being contested.

All this suggests a hypothesis. Maybe one function of serotonin—in human and nonhuman primates—is to regulate self-
esteem in accordance with social feedback; and maybe one function of self-esteem is, in turn, to help primates negotiate social
hierarchies, climbing as high on the ladder as circumstance permits. Self-esteem (read serotonin) keeps rising as long as one encounters social success, and each step in this elevation inclines one
to raise one's social sights a little higher. Variable self-esteem,
then, is evolution's way of preparing us to reach and maintain
whatever level of social status is realistic, given our various attributes (social skills, talent, etc.) and our milieu. High serotonin, in
this view, isn't nature's way of destining people from birth for
high status; it is nature's way of equipping any of us for high status
should we find ourselves possessing it. The flip side of this hypothesis is that low self-esteem (and low serotonin) is evolution's
way of equipping us for low status should our situation not be conducive to elevation.

This *doesn't* mean what an earlier generation of evolutionists
would have thought: that Mother Nature wants people with low
status to endure their fate patiently for "the greater good." Just
the opposite. A founding insight of evolutionary psychology is
that natural selection rarely designs things for the "good of the
group." Any psychological inclinations that offer a way to cope
with low status provide just that—a way to cope, a way to make
the best of a bad situation. The purpose of low self-esteem isn't
to bring submission for the sake of social order; more likely, its
purpose is to discourage people from conspicuously challenging
higher-status people who are, by virtue of their status, in a position to punish such insolence.

And what about the antisocial tendencies, the impulsive behavior linked with low serotonin in both human beings and monkeys? How does evolutionary psychology explain them? This is
where the demise of "good of the group" logic opens the way for
especially intriguing theories. In particular: primates may be designed to respond to low status by "breaking the rules" when they
can get away with it. The established social order isn't working
in their favor, so they circumvent its strictures at every opportunity. Similarly, inner-city thugs may be functioning as "designed":
their minds absorb environmental input reflecting their low socioeconomic standing and the absence of "legitimate" routes to

social elevation, and incline their behavior in the appropriately criminal direction.

The trouble with breaking rules, of course, is the risk of getting caught and punished. But, as Daly and Wilson note by quoting Bob Dylan, "When you ain't got nothin', you got nothin' to lose." In the environment of our evolution, low status often signified that a male had had little or no reproductive success to date; for such a male, taking risks to raise status could make sense in Darwinian terms. In hunter-gatherer societies, Daly and Wilson write, "competition can sometimes be fiercest near the bottom of the scale, where the man on track for total [reproductive] failure has nothing to lose by the most dangerous competitive tactics, and may therefore throw caution to the winds." Even as low self-esteem keeps him from challenging dominant males, he may behave recklessly toward those closer to him on the social ladder. Thus may the biochemistry of low status, along with the attendant states of mind, encourage impulsive risk-taking.

This theory, at any rate, would help make sense of some long-unexplained data. Psychologists found several decades ago that artificially lowering people's self-esteem—by giving them false reports about scores on a personality test—makes them more likely to cheat in a subsequent game of cards. Such risky rule-breaking is just the sort of behavior that makes more sense for a low-status animal than for a high-status animal.

To say that serotonin level is heavily influenced by social experience isn't to say that a person's genetic idiosyncrasies aren't significant. But it is to say that they are at best half the story. There are not yet any definitive studies on the "heritability" of serotonin level—the amount of the variation among people that is explained by genetic difference. But the one study that has been done suggests that less than half the variation in the population studied came from genetic differences, and the rest from differences in environment. And even this estimate of heritability is probably misleadingly high. Presumably, self-esteem correlates with many other personal attributes, such as physique or facial attractiveness. Impressive people, after all, inspire the sort of feedback that raises self-esteem and serotonin. Since these attributes are themselves quite heritable—traceable largely to a person's distinctive genes—some of the "heritability" estimate for serotonin may reflect genes not for high serotonin per se but for good looks, great body, and so on. (The technical term for this oblique genetic effect is "reactive heritability.")

At least some of the variation in serotonin level is grounded more directly in genetic difference. NIH researchers have identified a human gene that helps convert tryptophan, an amino acid found in some grains and fruits, into serotonin, and they have found a version of the gene that yields low serotonin levels. Still, there is no reason to believe that different ethnic groups have different genetic endowments for serotonin. Indeed, even if it turned out that American blacks on average had lower serotonin than whites, there would be no cause to implicate genes. One would expect groups that find themselves shunted toward the bottom of the socioeconomic hierarchy to have low serotonin. That may be nature's way of preparing them to take risks and to evade the rules of the powers that be.

This Darwinian theory integrating serotonin, status, and impulsive violence remains meagrely tested and is no doubt oversimplified. One complicating factor is modern life. People in contemporary America are part of various social hierarchies. An inner-city gang leader may get great, serotonin-boosting respect ("juice," as the suggestive street slang calls it) from fellow gang members while also getting serotonin-sapping signs of disrespect when he walks into a tony jewelry store, or even when he turns on the TV and sees that wealthy, high-status males tend to bear no physical or cultural resemblance to him. The human mind was designed for a less ambiguous setting—a hunter-gatherer society, in which a young man's social reference points stay fairly constant from day to day. We don't yet know how the mind responds to a world of wildly clashing status cues.

Another hidden complexity in this Darwinian theory lies in the fact that serotonin does lots of things besides mediate self-esteem and impulsive aggression. Precisely what it does depends on the part of the brain it is affecting and the levels of other neurotransmitters. Overall serotonin level is hardly the subtlest imaginable chemical index of a human being's mental state. Still, though we don't yet fathom the entire biochemistry of things like self-esteem, impulsiveness, and violence, there is little doubt among evolutionary psychologists that the subject is fathomable—and that it will get fathomed much faster if biomedical researchers, at NIH and elsewhere, start thinking in Darwinian terms.

If evolutionary psychologists are right in even the broad contours of their outlook, then there is good news and bad news for both Frederick Goodwin and Peter Breggin. For Goodwin, the good news is that his infamous remarks were essentially on target: he was right to compare violent inner-city males—or any other violent human males—to nonhuman primates (though he exaggerated the incidence of actual murder among such primates). The bad news is that his Violence Initiative, in failing to pursue that insight, in clinging to the view of violence as pathology, was doomed to miss a large part of the picture; the bulk of inner-city violence will probably never be explained by reference to head injuries, poor nutrition, prenatal exposure to drugs, and bad genes. If violence is a public-health problem, it is so mainly in the sense that getting killed is bad for your health.

Evolutionary psychology depicts all kinds of things often thought to be "pathological" as "natural": unyielding hatred, mild depression, a tendency of men to treat women as their personal property. Some Darwinians even think that rape may in some sense be a "natural" response to certain circumstances. Of course, to call these things "natural" isn't to call them beyond self-control, or beyond the influence of punishment. And it certainly isn't to call them good. If anything, evolutionary psychology might be invoked on behalf of the doctrine of Original Sin: we are in some respects born bad, and redemption entails struggle against our nature.

Many people, including many social scientists and biomedical researchers, seem to have trouble with the idea of a conflict between nature and morality. "I think this is a source of resistance to evolutionary ways of thinking," says John Tooby, a professor at the University of California at Santa Barbara, who along with his wife, Leda Cosmides, laid down some of the founding doctrines of evolutionary psychology. "There's a strong tendency to want to return to the romantic notion that the natural is the good." Indeed, "one modern basis for establishing morals is to try to ground them in the notion of sickness. Anything people don't like, they accuse the person doing it of being sick."

Thomas Szasz couldn't have said it better. Herein lies evolutionary psychology's good news for Peter Breggin: yes, it is indeed misleading to call most violence a pathology, a disorder. The bad news for Breggin is that, even though the causes of violence are broadly environmental, as he insists, they are nonetheless biological, because environmental forces are mediated biologically—in this case by, among other things, serotonin. Thus, a scientist can be a "biological determinist" or a "biological reductionist" without being a genetic determinist. He or she can say—as Daly and Wilson and Tooby and Cosmides do—that human behavior is driven by biological forces impinging on the brain, yet can view those forces largely as a reflection of a person's distinctive environment.

This confronts Breggin with a major rhetorical complication. Much of his success in arousing opposition to the Violence Initiative lay in conveniently conflating the terms "biological" and "genetic." He does this habitually. In suggesting that the initiative grew out of Goodwin's long-standing designs, Breggin says he has Baltimore *Evening Sun* articles from 1984 in which "Goodwin is talking about crime and violence being genetic and biological." In truth, these articles show Goodwin saying nothing about genes—only that violence has some biological correlates and might respond to pharmacological treatment. In Breggin's mind, "genetic" and "biological" are joined at the waist.

That these terms are not, in fact, inseparable—that something utterly biological, like serotonin level, may differ between two people because of environmental, not genetic, differences—poses a second problem for Breggin. The best way to illuminate the environmental forces he stresses may be to study the biological underpinnings of behavior, and that is a prospect he loathes. If serotonin is one chemical that converts poverty and disrespect into impulsiveness or aggression or low self-esteem, then it, along with other chemicals, may be a handy index of all these things—something whose level can be monitored more precisely than the things themselves. (Studies finding that blacks on average don't suffer from low self-esteem are based on asking black people and white people how they feel about themselves—a dubious approach, since expressions of humility seem to be more highly valued in white suburban culture than in black urban culture.)

That Breggin may be wrong in the way he thinks about biology and behavior doesn't mean that the unsettling scenarios he envisions are far-fetched. The government may well try to use biochemical "markers" to select violently inclined kids for therapy, or to screen prisoners for parole. (Then again, if these chemicals aren't simple "genetic markers," but rather are summaries of the way genes and environment have together molded a person's state of mind, how are they different from a standard psychological evaluation, which summarizes the same thing?) There may also be attempts to treat violently inclined teen-agers with serotonin-boosting drugs, as Breggin fears. And, though some teen-agers might thus be helped into the mainstream economy, these drugs could also become a palliative, a way to keep the inner city tranquil without improving it. The brave new world of biochemical diagnosis and therapy is coming; and, for all the insight evolutionary psychology brings, it won't magically answer the difficult questions that will arise.

The point to bear in mind is simply that less eerie, more traditionally liberal prescriptions for urban violence continue to make sense after we've looked at black teen-agers as animals—which, after all, is what human beings are. The view from evolutionary psychology suggests that one way to reduce black violence would be to make the inner cities places where young men have nonviolent routes to social status and the means and motivation to follow them. Better-paying jobs, and better public schools, for example, wouldn't hurt. Oddly enough, thinking about genes from a Darwinian standpoint suggests that inner-city teen-agers are victims of their environment.

WHAT TO DO ABOUT CRIME[4]

Blaming Crime on Root Causes

Crime is a subject akin to, "What is wrong with the Boston Celtics and the Chicago Cubs?" Everyone has an opinion, and I want to give you as many opportunities as you need to express those opinions. Much of what I am going to say is drawn from the last chapter of the book that I edited with Joan Petersilia, *Crime*, with preceding chapters written by other scholars, some of whom I agree with, but all distinguished in their field.

[4]Speech delivered by James Q. Wilson, a James Collins Professor of Management at UCLA, on Jan. 19, 1995, at the Independent Policy Forum Luncheon, San Francisco, CA, from *Vital Speeches of the Day* 61/12:373 Ap 1 '95. Copyright © 1995 by The Independent Institute. Reprinted with permission.

When we think about crime, we must realize that this nation faces not one crime problem, but two. The first is a problem that is nearly universal, affecting virtually all industrialized societies. It is the enormous increase in the rate of property crime that has occurred since the late 1950's.

Today, the United States does not stand alone as the most crime-ridden industrialized nation in the world. It stands shoulder to shoulder with Sweden, Germany, Spain, England, Wales and the Netherlands as one of many crime-ridden nations. Today, the burglary rate is about as high in Sweden as it is in the United States. The chances of having your car stolen are about the same in London as they are in New York City. The drug problem is everywhere. These facts must reflect some profound cultural change in the West, a cultural change for which I doubt there are any governmental solutions.

The United States, however, does stand alon[e] in one respect, and that is our second crime problem, the problem of violence and especially juvenile violence. Beginning about 1985, coincident with the advent of crack cocaine on the streets of many large American cities, juvenile homicide rates, that had been declining for five years (as adult homicide rates had been declining for five years), began to escalate. Between 1985 and 1990, the juvenile homicide rate for white youths increased by about 50%, and among African-American youths it tripled. There are some indications, in the last few months, that these rates of violent crime, particularly among juveniles, have begun to come down. But, if they do come down, I doubt very much that they will ever come down to the low levels they were once at—what now seems in retrospect to be the "benign 1960's."

When we think about the problem of solving crime, therefore, we have to be clear about which one we're trying to solve. The first problem, the universal property crime problem, is one that we each "solve" by means of personal protection. We make ourselves prisoners in our own home. We lock up everything we have. We hire private security guards. The second problem, that of rising levels of juvenile violence, demands a different approach. In thinking about this subject, most people find themselves divided into one of two camps: those who believe that we must attack the root causes of crime, and those who believe that we must employ the criminal justice system. Of course everyone who thinks about this might say we should do a bit of both, but in the area of crime, as with "What's wrong with the Boston Celtics?", people have very firm views. We each have an ideology on this matter that makes us akin to the man holding a hammer for whom all the world looks like a nail. We either wish to use punishment because we are punitive, or we wish to attack root causes because we consider ourselves tender-hearted.

What can we say about these two approaches? First, with respect to punishment there are certain myths that Americans have allowed themselves to believe that I believe ought to be dispelled. It is often said, for example, that the United States imprisons more people in proportion to its population than any other country except South Africa and the former Soviet Union. This statement is false. Worse than false, it is meaningless because the key issue is not how many people in proportion to the population are in prison but what proportion of crimes committed lead to incarceration. If you look at violent crime rates, our use of prison is not very different from that to be found in Canada, England, or Australia. With respect to property crimes, we *do* use prison more frequently than England and Sweden, and that may be one of the reasons why their property crime rates are going up while our property crime rates are going down.

A second myth is that we have increased dramatically the number of people in prison and gotten nothing in return. Crime, it is said, has remained high despite escalating prison populations. This is a proposition that cannot be conclusively tested because we cannot conduct a controlled experiment in which half the states imprison people, the other half do not, and we observe the consequences. But it is a fact that coincident with rising prison population there began in 1979–80, a steep reduction in the crime rate as reported by the victimization surveys. This reduction in the crime rate was, I believe, the result of three factors: First, the population was getting older, but this only explains a small part of the decline. Second, there was an increase in the probability of going to prison and this increased the deterrent value of the criminal justice system. Third, the aggregate number of people in prison increased the incapacitation value of the criminal justice system even though time served in state prison has been going down more or less steadily for 40 years. In the 1950's, the median burglar released from prison in the United States served 24 months. By 1985, that figure was down to 14 months, even though the median burglar today has typically a much longer rap sheet than the median burglar of 30 years ago. By contrast, England and Sweden have been reducing the probability of going to prison, and their crime rates have been going up. We cannot prove from that correlation that less prison has caused more crime, but at least we can say that these relationships are not consistent with the proposition that we have purchased nothing by our increase in the prison population.

However, there are some limitations to prison which need to be examined seriously. One is the fact that until 1985, only about 8% of the inmates of state prisons were drug offenders. Today 25% are, and in the federal system, the percentage is over 60%. We began to take the matter seriously owing to the advent of crack cocaine and the complaints in neighborhoods about crack dealing and the juvenile violence associated with it. We have dramatically increased the use of prison for drug offenders, and we cannot be certain what we have purchased because drug offending, unlike armed robbery or homicide, is a business, and if you take one dealer off the street, one or more dealers will rise up to take his place. It is my view that if you wish to control drug abuse, you must reduce demand. It is my view that prison or other forms of punishment must be part of a demand-reduction strategy, because young people ordinarily will not voluntarily remain in drug treatment programs. Whether the use of prison space is the best way to link sanctions to a drug demand-reduction strategy is unclear, and a good deal of creative thought needs to be devoted to the question of how best to make demand-reduction strategies effective.

Another criticism of our increased use of prison is that it has not adequately addressed the juvenile problem, and I believe that this is correct. I believe that young people are calculating, just as older people are calculating, and sometimes they calculate with far greater precision than we. Nonetheless, it remains the case that young persons are more impulsive than older ones and thus distant penalties are less likely to make a difference. Moreover, because of the conditions in inner-city communities owing to the escalation of gang violence and its association with crack dealing, gun ownership has become necessary in the eyes of many juveniles for reasons of self-defense. The situation in many inner-city neighborhoods is not radically different from that in Beirut or Bosnia. Finally, young people have, like all people, a demand for respect. When respect is no longer given by the conventional sources or when those conventional sources are themselves no longer highly regarded, respect may take the form of exaggerated manhood—the ability to display force and use it credibly, and the ability to wear proudly the fact that one has done time in juvenile hall. For all of these reasons, we have not yet adequately accessed the role the criminal justice system can play in controlling the most explosive part of our crime problem, juvenile violence.

Let me turn now to the subject of root causes. Some of you may know that I am not a great admirer of most "root cause" theories of crime. It turns out that what many people who have this view mean by "root causes" are those things that they don't like about society. If they can blame crime on these factors, perhaps they can get more government efforts directed at those things. The difficulty is that though there is some relationship between poverty and crime, it is not a very close one. There is only a very weak relationship between crime and unemployment or the business cycle. There are many good reasons for trying to do something about poverty and providing jobs, but ending crime is the worse possible reason. Indeed, much of the increase in crime around the world has occurred at a time of enormous gains in national prosperity and national well-being, so much so that in this century, unlike in the previous century, the crime rate has become unhinged from the business cycle. Crime is more likely to go up in periods of prosperity today than it is in periods of depression—a reversal of the situation that existed, so far as we can tell, in the previous century.

But there are root causes of crime even though they are sometimes misidentified. These causes are *family* and *neighborhood*. We are beginning now for the first time to talk candidly about family conditions in the United States. For some time in the 60's and 70's, people who criticized single-parent families or out-of-wedlock births were themselves criticized for stigmatizing an "alternative lifestyle" or an "alternative family arrangement," as if all family arrangements were equally valid, and one could choose among them the way you may choose among Ben & Jerry's ice-cream flavors. But, *the family* as we know it, as indeed every culture in every civilization in the world now knows it, is the product of tens of thousands of years of evolution and painful trial-and-error. The only family that has survived the test of this evolutionary experience has been the two-parent family, sometimes extended, sometimes nuclear, but always with a father and mother, always with a marital commitment designed to preserve and enhance the well-being of the child.

There are now data that show any fair-minded observer rather conclusively that after controlling for income, and for every racial or ethnic group, children raised in single-parent families headed by never-married young women, are materially worse off in terms of school achievements, delinquency, emotional problems. These risks are greater for boys than for girls.

If this is the case, then we ought not to think of the problem of family structure as a black problem, a white problem, or a problem of any particular color. It transcends color and affects all segments of society. Nor should we think of it simply as a problem of financial support because, except at the very highest income level, a level achieved among women only by "Murphy Brown" and a few others, a child raised in a never-married mother's home is materially worse off. What can we do about this? As many politicians have said, accurately, *governments don't raise children, families do*. Nonetheless, government policy can create conditions in which families are more or less likely to be healthy. We have created conditions in which families are less likely to be healthy. I do not assert that the existence of the Aid to Families with Dependent Children program (AFDC) or welfare has caused an increase in illegitimacy. I do believe it has helped make it possible, but I do not believe that it is the sole cause. Nor do I believe that the business cycle is the sole cause. If you try to explain the growth of single-parent families from the early 1960's until today, it turns out that neither economic factors nor changes in the inflation-adjusted value of welfare payments can explain more than a part of the increase.

The culture has changed, not only here but abroad. The stigma attached to an out-of-wedlock birth has gone. The sense that a male who has impregnated a female has an obligation, enforceable either by law, custom, or by the female's tough brothers, to marry the young woman has been profoundly weakened. As a consequence, young men now have at a young age what they always wanted, action and no commitment. Young girls want something else. I am not suggesting that young girls are uninterested in action, but most would like a separate household as well, out from under the thumb of their parents. Many of them would like babies because they find babies appealing, and they want to care for them. But, having grown up in a household headed by a young unmarried woman who herself got pregnant at an early age, having now gotten pregnant at an early age in her own case, they discover government programs that promise, via AFDC, food stamps, housing subsidies, and Medicaid, that they can have an independent household. They often jump at the chance and take some delight in the fact that they can do this without the services of a male to assist them. The ones who lose are the children.

In my view, the current national debate over welfare reform is miscast. It is miscast because of the phrase, "welfare reform." Many people believe that what is at stake here is how many tax dollars are being spent on enabling poor people not to work. Now these matters *are* at stake, but there is something more fundamental here and that is *the well-being of these children*—children who are the unintended victims of a culture that no longer produces with much surety intact, two-parent families whose concern is the well-being of children. How can government change this? One view says that we can change it by going cold turkey: "Let's end all welfare! Throw people on general county relief if necessary, but send the unmistakable message that you cannot use public money to support the consequences of your sexual indiscretions." That may work, almost surely in the long run *would* work, but at what cost we do not know. Then there are those who say that welfare recipients must work to earn their welfare payments. That may be a desirable goal, but one has to ask whether we really want the mothers of newborn infants working when there is not another parent at home to take care of the child. Do we wish to move from single-parent families to no-parent families? Possibly, but I doubt it.

A third alternative is to say, "What can we do to supply an adequate environment for these children?" Our goal should be to alter expectations, so that boys will not grow up believing that sexual exploitation and the reputation thereby acquired is their main object, and girls will not think that sexual experimentation leading to the formation of independent households is their goal. Boys and girls will grow up thinking that romance and commitment and marriage are the goals they ought to seek. One possibility is to create arrangements whereby young girls who are pregnant, without a husband and who apply for welfare are told that they may have all the benefits provided they do not set up an independent household. This might mean living with their own parents. In some cases of course, their own parents are either abusive or have been proved incompetent. One alternative would be improved adoption laws, making it easier to adopt, even transracially. Another alternative would be the use of family shelters or group homes in which the mother and her child would live, so that real adults who really understand how children have to be cared for will be supervising the behavior of young girls who in many cases do not know this. There would be no drugs, no alcohol, and no boyfriends on the premises.

You may think that this is a radically new idea, but it is as old as the country itself. The Florence Crittendon Homes have been doing this for decades. There are family shelters in every part of this country. They have been doing it with private money, as charities. When the 800-pound gorilla called government walks into the middle of the room, it ignores history, ignores private initiatives, and says, "We know best." Liberals want to give the women the money without any strings attached, conservatives want to make the women work for it. But neither ask, what will this do to the child? How can such children be saved? What lessons have we learned from history as to how to do it better?

I believe that welfare reform ought to be linked to crime control, and we ought to understand that the two are part of an indissoluble whole. I believe that this might help the acute American problem of juvenile violence. I am not convinced that it would help the worldwide problem of property crime. In other countries, we have many different kinds of welfare systems, yet they, too, have rapidly escalating rates of property crime and drug abuse. I have no idea how to deal with that large problem. That is a problem of Western culture, at this particular time in its development.

Has Western culture, born with the enthusiasm, excitement and insight of the Enlightenment of the 18th century, having given us economic prosperity, technological advancement, scientific invention, material progress, and personal freedom, exhausted its moral capital? Our critics in this world, in Islamic nations, and Confucian nations, are watching us, and they believe we have made the wrong decision. I don't believe that we have made the wrong decision; I believe that a free people in a prosperous economy have enormous capacities for self-correction that are not available to less-free people. In the next century, we will find out whether I am right.

COPS & COMMUNITY[5]

The Parkside Motel in St. Petersburg, Florida, is not the sort of place you'd want to come to on a family vacation. A dilapidated motor court that rents "weekly efficiencies" and is just a few steps shy of a flophouse, it sits on the edge of Harbordale, one of the drug-ridden south-side neighborhoods that complicate St. Petersburg's image as a sedate haven for retirees from the Midwest.

On an unseasonably cool and overcast day, Officer Holly Hadrika pulls her patrol car onto the grass in front of the Parkside to stop and question a young woman with a gold braid who matches the description of a suspect in a knifepoint burglary the month before. The woman, who had been walking down the street toward the motel, tells Hadrika with perfect aplomb that she doesn't know how to spell her own name and can't remember her last address, blaming her confusion on years of drinking. She says the manager at the Parkside can vouch for her if he's there, but he may not be, because he lives off-site.

Hadrika nods, expressionless, and, leaving the woman with two other cops who have joined them, heads inside to talk with the manager. "What she doesn't know," Hadrika says with a slight smile, "is that I probably speak with the manager at least once a day. And he lives right here."

It is the suspect's misfortune to have been stopped by the one police officer in St. Petersburg who can tell on the spot that she's lying. Hadrika is Harbordale's community police officer, one of 52 who are each responsible for a patch of the city's turf. She has spent three years in the neighborhood, day in and day out. She knows its drug dealers and addicts, its schoolchildren and troubled families. She knows the efficiency motel regulars and their companions, the apartment managers who will cooperate with her and the ones who won't, the property owners who let dealers work out of their houses and the homeowners who will turn out to help her fight dealers on their block. In turn, many of them—dealers, schoolchildren, managers and homeowners alike—know her. Hadrika is sure that the woman she has stopped is from out-

[5]Article by Rob Gurwitt from *Governing* 8/8:16-24 My '95. Copyright © 1995 by *Governing*. Reprinted with permission.

side the neighborhood, which the Parkside's manager confirms: He's seen her around a few times, he says, but doesn't know much about her.

Back out front, the woman's luck has vanished entirely. Sandy Minor, the community police officer for the next area over, is talking quietly with a woman who was passing by—one of her neighborhood contacts and, as it happens, the burglary victim. The victim identifies Hadrika's suspect. "I think," says Minor, drily, "we've got probable cause to arrest."

The St. Petersburg police have been engaged in community policing since 1990, and at its heart, it comes down to this: In every neighborhood in the city, the police department has at least one officer who either knows the terrain intimately or is learning it. These are not, as the community policing stereotype would have it, cops walking a beat. They are more like roving problem-solvers—policing their neighborhoods "the way they would want if they lived there," as Princeton University's John DiIulio puts it. They find ways to shut down drug houses and chase dealers from neglected corners; they enlist community help in everything from dealing with troublemakers to cleaning up the neighborhood; they find and try to resolve difficulties of all sorts—from elderly homeowners who can no longer keep their property in shape to teenagers who attract the wrong crowd—before these problems kick a street into a downward spiral. And they put what they have learned to use, as Hadrika's suspect has just discovered, in catching criminals.

The results have been encouraging. Both the crime rate and residents' fear of crime have dropped in the years since community policing was established in St. Petersburg. Many of the city's neighborhoods have become fiercely protective of their community police, finding them office space to work out of and even buying them bicycles when the department's budget falls short. In neighborhoods where police were long seen as little more than an occupying army, they have built up levels of trust that would have been unthinkable a decade ago. "St. Petersburg," says Dennis C. Smith, who directs the public policy program at New York University's graduate school of public policy, "has taken community policing as far or further than any place I've seen."

Yet St. Petersburg's very success also points up how difficult community policing can be to do well. For as the program has taken hold, the role of officers like Holly Hadrika and her colleagues has expanded beyond law enforcement: They have become de facto community organizers, social workers and civic ombudsmen. They have, in short, been thrust into the vanguard of the city's efforts to shore up and reclaim neighborhood life.

There are plenty of police chiefs around the country who believe that is exactly where the police ought to be. "What we want is to enhance and nurture the neighborhood concept of churches, schools, stores, people interacting, festivities, cultural diversity," says Nicholas Pastore, the chief of police in New Haven, Connecticut. "To do that, people need to feel safe in the effort. You'll find that most people want to move in that direction, but they want help overcoming their fears."

Making that happen, however, turns out to require much more than a police department dedicated to the idea. If, as is happening in St. Petersburg and in other cities, police officers are being asked to stand in the way not simply of criminals but of the forces that drive crime and neighborhood decay, then they need help. And they need it not just from the community, as any community police officer can tell you, but from the one place it can be most difficult to find: the rest of city government.

"We're asking our officers to take on the issues that create an environment of crime and violence and fear," says Darrel Stephens, St. Petersburg's soft-spoken chief of police and a nationally known community policing theorist. "Those are very complex issues. In the past we told our citizens, 'Give us resources and taxes, and we'll solve these problems ourselves.' We've learned it's not possible to do that. We won't significantly change neighborhoods, stop them from decline and help rebuild them unless we have the participation both of people in the neighborhood and of the rest of government."

There are, it is true, plenty of opportunities for St. Petersburg's community police, acting alone, to make a difference. Driving through Coquina Key, a racially mixed neighborhood a bit to the south of Harbordale, Officer Terrell Skinner points to several houses where single mothers, away at work all day and often into the evening, had lost control of adolescent children whose raucous activities were driving neighbors to put their houses up for sale. He helped the women get blanket trespass warnings limiting visitors while they were out and giving Skinner the ability to crack down on any violators. "The 'For Sale' signs," he says, "went away."

On the north side of town, Officer Mark Blackwood has made
a point of getting to know the youngsters in the middle-class
neighborhood he covers, hanging out with them while they play,
buying lemonade from their stands in the summer, helping the
parents of a handful of kids experimenting with LSD find places
for them in drug programs. So when two boys threw a stink bomb
through an elderly resident's mail slot, setting her rug on fire,
Blackwood knew within a day who had done it; he took them,
with their parents, over to the woman's house the following evening to sit down and talk about how to make amends. "The kids
in my neighborhood pimp each other out to him in a second," says
Lieutenant Tony Potts, who directs St. Petersburg's community
policing program and lives in the area for which Blackwood is responsible.

All told, there are 48 community police areas in St. Petersburg, and within them, officers have broad latitude to deal with
whatever problems they and local residents think are priorities.
That can be anything from making life difficult for drug dealers—Hadrika and Minor are jokingly referred to around police
headquarters as "Cagney and Lacey" for their hard-nosed attitude toward the dealers in their neighborhoods—to setting up a
program to identify elderly residents with Alzheimer's disease
who get confused and wander from home.

It doesn't take long, though, to realize that for all the community police officers' autonomy, the ultimate resolution of a problem is often out of their hands. You get an inkling of why just a
few minutes after Hadrika's burglar is handcuffed and sitting in
the back seat of the patrol car on the way back to police headquarters. Searching her pockets, Hadrika turns up a crack pipe; the
woman tells her that she's been using the drug since Christmas.
She can't, she says quietly, get off it.

Stopped at a light, Hadrika turns her head. "Do you want to
get help?" The woman tells her she's been unable to.

"You've got to ask the judge," Hadrika tells her, stressing
each word. "You have to ask the judge to help you out."

The problem, Hadrika later explains, is that in St. Petersburg, as elsewhere, the number of people wanting to get into
drug rehab programs is far greater than the space available.
About the only way to make sure it happens these days is to get
a court order. Every so often, people who've gotten to know Hadrika in Harbordale will tell her they have a drug problem, even

try to get her to arrest them, in hopes that she can help them get into a program. If the woman Hadrika has just arrested doesn't get into drug rehab, it's a pretty good bet that her path will cross Hadrika's again.

The fact is, community police officers have to rely on other agencies and government officials daily. Getting vacant houses boarded up or trash-strewn lots cleaned may be problems that neighborhood residents ask the police to resolve, but it's actually the sanitation department or code enforcement officers who must make sure it happens. Putting pressure on a motel owner who has been catering to prostitutes and their trade depends on the willingness of other city officials, from fire inspectors to nuisance-abatement boards, to help out. Getting a handle on public drunkenness can take anything from finding alcohol treatment programs with available slots to working with liquor control authorities to shut down troublesome outlets.

All of this is an inevitable result of a major strand of the thought that underlies community policing. It was laid out in an influential 1982 article in *The Atlantic* by Professors James Q. Wilson, now at UCLA, and George Kelling, now at Northeastern University. Titled "Broken Windows," the article made the point that crime is linked to a disorderly environment and that allowing signs of disorder—graffiti, a broken window—to go untended promotes the impression that no one cares about the neighborhood, which in turn permits crime to breed. Reducing crime and the fear of crime, Kelling and Wilson suggested, would depend on a "return to our long-abandoned view that the police ought to protect communities as well as individuals. . . . [T]he police—and the rest of us—ought to recognize the importance of maintaining, intact, communities without broken windows."

In the years since then, most of the academic and professional discussion of community policing has focused on just this issue: moving beyond the simple question of apprehending criminals to the infinitely more complex questions of managing public order. Even if there are no definitive blueprints, police administrators are now keenly aware of such tasks as restructuring the department to support its community-oriented functions and finding ways to involve community groups and ordinary citizens in identifying and resolving problems plaguing their neighborhoods.

What has gotten less attention, however, is the question of coordinating with other government agencies, which Kelling and

Wilson, in a later article, warned might be the most difficult challenge of all. "The police can bring problems to the attention of other city agencies," they wrote, "but the system is not always organized to respond."

That is a widely held view. "One of the problems with community policing in most cities is that it's a police department program, not a government program or a particular chief executive's program," says Wesley Skogan, professor of political science and urban affairs at Northwestern University in Chicago. "This is really fatal, because one of the things about community policing is that it inevitably calls for a big expansion of the police mandate to cover a broad range of disorder, decay and quality-of-life issues as well as crime fighting."

Perhaps the single most admired city in the country in community policing circles is Portland, Oregon, where the program has lasted through several changes in both police and city administration. One clear reason for its success there is that the city bureaucracy has been geared for some time to respond to neighborhood concerns—crafting a coordinated response to particular problems, while it still takes work, is not the alien endeavor in Portland that it can be in other cities. "If police agencies are forced to facilitate projects without assistance, they'll fail," says Tom Peavey, a neighborhood resource officer in the city's Central District. "When police have to pull their resources and go to another project—since they can't do everything at once—if there's no set structure of community service providers or public agencies to maintain what was created, then pretty soon it'll be business as usual."

Far more common than Portland are cases such as Houston, which was the first big-league city to embrace community policing, under former Chief Lee Brown. The city, which drew widespread attention in the 1980s for its efforts, is now drawing equal attention for its rejection of the whole idea. Under Chief Sam Nuchia, the police there have adopted a strategy focused explicitly on fighting crime—boosted by the addition of more than 600 police officers since the beginning of 1992—with a combination of aggressive patrol and investigations, rapid response times, arresting parole violators and saturating the city's highest crime beats with additional patrol units. Community policing in Houston is dead.

But the fact is, Houston's experiment with it was, at best, limited. For one thing, police leaders never tried to train officers in the new discipline or to rearrange the department to maximize their effectiveness. Just as ruinous, although less noticed by outsiders, they never got the rest of city government to buy in to their efforts.

"One of the frustrations in Houston was that we were a police department all by ourselves," says Elizabeth Watson, who followed Brown as chief there before moving on to take that post in Austin, Texas. "Many of the things we encountered were things over which we had no control: lighting, weeds, graffiti, the deteriorating conditions that can breed a criminal element. It was very difficult for the police to work in concert with city government."

The problem, Watson argues, was that community policing demands coordination, when the norm is for agencies to focus solely on their own priorities. "Each department establishes its own directions; it hears its own drummer," she says. "It's a natural development, and it takes a lot of hard work on a continuing basis to overcome that natural tendency." Indeed, many cities don't seem up to the task. A recent study by the Vera Institute of Justice in New York found that, in seven of the eight cities with community policing that it analyzed, coordination between the police and other municipal agencies had failed entirely.

There are signs, though, that things may be changing. Roberta Lesh, who conducts training sessions on policing issues for the International City/County Management Association, says that recently the city officials she deals with have been showing more recognition of the role they can play in dealing with crime and violence. "It doesn't take a mental genius to figure out that the police can't operate in a vacuum," she says, "so we're beginning to see this shift around the country, where managers and elected officials are not just thinking of it as a police issue."

In Austin, for instance, where Elizabeth Watson is getting ready to reorganize the entire police department to focus on the city's neighborhoods, the city administration is also gearing up to make it easier for each neighborhood to work directly with its various departments. And in Chicago, which has undertaken what may be the country's most ambitious effort to re-gear a police department for community policing, the improvement of city services in coordination with police "beat teams" has been part of the program from the start. Indeed, Mayor Richard M. Daley kicked the whole program off with a now-famous meeting in which he told his department heads that community policing was his policy and that if they didn't support it they'd lose their jobs. He has kept the heat on by having service requests generated by beat teams and the citizens they work with coordinated through his office.

St. Petersburg could easily have gone the way of Houston. Although the advent of community policing there coincided with growing concern among some officials at city hall about the deteriorating state of the neighborhoods, the city's attention for the most part lay elsewhere. As in many other places, local officials in St. Pete—backed by most of the city's major financial interests and its only newspaper, the *St. Petersburg Times*—spent the 1970s and 1980s all but fixated on downtown development. By the beginning of this decade, the city had an empty $135 million domed stadium (it will be filled only with the start of the 1998 baseball season), the equally empty Bay Plaza commercial development downtown, and a rising tide of resentment among residents who felt they'd been ignored for too long. "There were bumps at the highest levels," says Planning Director Ralph Stone. "The city manager was used to dealing with things set by the council's agenda, which really lagged behind neighborhood needs."

All of that changed in 1993, when an electoral revolt was touched off by the police chief who brought community policing to the city. Ernest Curtsinger came to St. Petersburg from Los Angeles, where his direction of a community policing pilot project in the high-profile Wilshire District had given him a reputation as an innovator. He was an immediate hit with the St. Petersburg force, combining as he did the hard-nosed fervor for crime-fighting that has been the LAPD trademark with a devotion to giving his officers far more of a say in how the department ran than they had ever been accustomed to.

"He was our savior," says Sam Giardina, a 23-year veteran and former police union president who is now a community police officer on the western edge of the city's downtown business district. "He made us feel like adults again. When he went to community policing, he told us, 'This is your area. You will get to know the people, you'll work whatever hours you need, and you don't need me to tell you how to do your job.'" In an organization that had been as hierarchical and tightly controlled as any, Curtsinger's insistence that community police officers be fettered only by their imaginations and the bounds of the law was almost revolutionary.

But his actions had another, even more far-reaching consequence. Placing community police officers around the city—with orders to listen carefully to the residents in their areas and then do something about their concerns—turned out to be a revelation to the neighborhoods. To many of them, Curtsinger's shift to community policing marked the first time in years that a branch of city government was not only paying attention to them but giving them a voice in what went on in their bounds. "The neighborhoods had been slighted for many, many years," says Karen Mullins, president of the city's Council of Neighborhood Associations. "He changed that."

So when Curtsinger was accused of insensitivity toward his black officers and toward the black community in general, the city's white, middle-class neighborhoods rallied around him. And when he was ultimately dismissed by an acting city manager, resentment boiled over: Angry citizens placed an initiative on the ballot to replace the council-manager system with a strong mayor, while Curtsinger himself ran for mayor against David Fischer, who had held the post under the old system. In a closely fought and often bitter campaign, the strong-mayor initiative won but Curtsinger lost.

The message, however, got through. Fischer, like Curtsinger, ran on a pro-neighborhoods plank, and since taking office he has pushed aggressively to steer the city's resources toward its neighborhoods. Even before the change in government, the planning department had begun working with one run-down neighborhood on a plan to improve its infrastructure and deal with the growing number of properties in the area that were attracting prostitutes; it expected to take two years to put the plan into effect. Fischer, on taking office, announced to his department heads that he wanted a full-bore commitment on the part of every city agency to turn the neighborhood around, and gave them six months. Since then, the city has moved on to six other neighborhoods with similarly concerted efforts to overhaul them.

In each of those, community police officers have played a central role. They are part of so-called "city teams" that bring together staff from the planning, codes, housing and public works departments with responsibility for a particular neighborhood.

They work with bankers, real estate brokers, neighborhood leaders and other city officials to find ways of bringing new investments into hard-hit neighborhoods. And they have driven an ongoing process of change in municipal procedures and ordinances designed to strengthen the hand of the police in dealing with problems, from an open-container law to help them rid the downtown business district of public drunkenness to a new lot-cleaning program aimed at clearing problem properties far more quickly than in the past.

The community police have given the entire city establishment a point of entry into its neighborhoods. Because many—though not all—of the officers are the most trusted city officials in their neighborhoods, they lend credibility to the city's development efforts. "What we're doing couldn't exist and be effective without community policing," says Mike Dove, who directs St. Petersburg's neighborhood programs. "It's a lot easier to work in a neighborhood where the community police officer has established him- or herself. People get a more comfortable feeling working with them than with the typical bureaucrat. They already see their CPO as a problem-solver."

After years of getting little but good press all over the country, community policing lately has run into more questions. There is, for one thing, the issue of its cost: A number of cities have found it necessary to hire additional patrol officers to replace the officers they assign to neighborhood detail—although others, including St. Petersburg, have managed to avoid that expense. There is also the persistent problem that, in the majority of cities where the officers who respond to 911 calls are different from community officers, there is tension between the two parts of the force. Even in St. Petersburg, where CPOs make a habit of giving arrest credit to patrol officers, the problem endures. "We still have the let's-bust-bad-guys group," says Tony Potts, "and the fact is, we want them, because we still do that. But we also want them to see that we need to do both things. We've gone through some rocky roads on that."

There is also the larger issue, for a country obsessed with getting tough on crime, of whether community policing can deliver results as quickly as most communities and politicians would like. "What we have mostly done is prove that the assumptions underlying the old model don't work," says NYU's Dennis Smith, a community policing advocate. "We have yet to demonstrate that the new model does work."

And perhaps most difficult of all, there is the question of whether the new, community-oriented roles being thrust on police officers in cities such as St. Petersburg are the most appropriate use of people with a badge and a gun. As a society, we have been grappling with the forces of urban decay for decades. Why should the police be any better at resolving them than social workers or urban redevelopment authorities have proven to be?

The answer lies, in part, in the notion that all the police are doing is finding new ways of filling their traditional role: keeping communities safe. There is strong evidence from St. Petersburg and other cities—in the form of both surveys and anecdotal confirmation—that community policing helps residents feel safer, and certainly more connected to the police department. "I firmly believe that one police officer can make a difference in a neighborhood," says Darrel Stephens. "It may not be a change-the-world difference, but it's a difference that makes things a little better, a little easier to live, a little more civil, a little less fear, maybe less actual crime."

The result is that the police create room for other forces to take hold. By reducing the fear of crime or violence in a neighborhood, they give neighborhood associations the confidence they need to begin mobilizing residents, they give city agencies on-the-ground support, and they make it more likely that the kind of private money needed to turn a neighborhood around will ultimately show up. "It's not a question of the police opening a grocery store," says Drew Diamond, the former chief of police in Tulsa, Oklahoma, and now director of operations for the Community Policing Consortium in Washington, D.C., "but being part of a broader community process that enables that to happen."

That is why, if community police officers in St. Petersburg are dependent on other city agencies to help them do their work, the reverse is also true. "I would advise any city that's contemplating revitalizing neighborhoods by geographical area like we have, make sure you've got community policing first," says David Fischer. "Because security, and believing that you can secure the place, are prerequisites to doing this."

"Community-based police officers need to understand their role in society, and that role is no longer the crime fighter who chases the bad guy and goes red-lights-and-sirens," says Bob Taylor, a one-time Portland cop who has studied community policing as director of the research office at the University of Texas at Tyler. "It's looking at deep-rooted social problems in the neighborhood, figuring out how to deal with the way people live, what resources they can tap into, how to look at cleaning up the surrounding environment of the neighborhood. Those are things we've never talked about in policing, and it's an extremely big order to fill. On the other hand, who else could fulfill it?"

III. SOLUTIONS

EDITOR'S INTRODUCTION

Study after study has shown that crime in the United States is concentrated in the neighborhoods with the worst schools, the most poverty, and the highest rates of unemployment, as well as the highest rates of alcohol and drug addiction. Research has also shown that in such areas there is often a feeling of alienation from, and animosity toward, those whose job it is to serve and protect the community—most specifically, the police. But there is hope. There are solutions. New Orleans, a city plagued by a crippling crime rate, has organized a Community Oriented Policing Squad, known as COPS, to patrol, on foot, one of that city's most dangerous areas. The 45 cops assigned to the program got to know the residents, helped keep the area free from trash, prevented graffiti, and rounded up kids who played hookey from school. By the end of 1995 killings in those areas had dropped 75 percent. Richard Lacayo, writing for *Time*, tells us that New Orleans is not alone: the crime rate is decreasing across the country—thanks to an aggressive "war on crime."

However, police intervention is not enough to end crime. Tucker Carlson in *Policy Review* quotes statistics showing that a staggering number of crimes are committed by those either on parole or on probation. Since anonymity has been shown to be a significant factor in many crimes, Carlson believes that the simple act of informing a community when an ex-con moves into the neighborhood can deter further criminal acts. He adds further that in some places where this has been tried, the community has actually helped to rehabilitate the offender by offering the support system needed to begin a new life. Jeremy Rabkin in the *New Republic* tells us that in order to fight crime we must revise our system of punishment, not intensify it. He explains that the end result of such a large number of people being pushed through the criminal justice system is the re-creation on the street of the violent prison subculture. His solution: we must view safety as a right and demand payment from our government for "defaulting on its obligation to protect citizens." Another suggestion comes to us from Robert Dillon in *Los Angeles*. He explores the idea of hand guns as a deterent to crime—a notion which occurred to him after his son was shot near his own "safe" neighborhood. Still another possible solution—this time in the form of drug legalization—comes from *The Washington Monthly*. The benefits of legalization would, according to the article, range from controlling the quality of these often poisonous substances to freeing up the legal and prison systems to deal with more violent criminals.

In an article called "Crime and Punishment," Ted Gest and his colleagues argue that while incarceration has only a limited effect on crime, that effect may be increased by taking certain steps to improve the prison system. Anne Morrison Piehl and John DiIulio also consider the usefulness of prison as a rehabilitation tool and as a preventive measure in their *Brookings* article "Does Prison Pay?" Revisited.

Finally, pursuing the subject of prevention, *Education Digest* outlines steps that can be taken in our communities and in our schools to keep young people from falling into the "crime trap."

LAW AND ORDER[1]

Want to see a civic monument that no city would ever want? Go to New Orleans and proceed to the intersection of Congress and Law streets, just a few blocks from the tourists' Latin Quarter. Walk anywhere in that neighborhood of trashed storefronts and blunt-shouldered housing projects. It won't take long to find walls that are spattered with grimy little craters. Those are bullet holes. Every one of them is an unofficial memorial to the mayhem that was daily life around there until not so long ago.

Starting in the late 1980s, drug dealers had claimed the place as their own, part sales ground, part killing ground, where they seized market share the hard way, with drive-by shootings and turf wars. At the nearby St. Philip Social Service Center, preschoolers learned to dive for the floor in "shooting drills," then stay there until their teachers sounded the all clear. By 1994

[1]Article by Richard Lacayo from *Time* 147/3:48-54 Ja '96. Copyright © 1996 by TIME INC. Reprinted with permission.

there were three or more killings each month on the streets outside. Standing now where the unthinkable used to be the unre-
markable, police lieutenant Edwin Compass III looks around with
a shudder. "I'd bet it was the most dangerous block in the U.S."

The good thing about monuments is they commemorate the
past. Last year the city inaugurated a Communuity Oriented
Policing Squad (COPS), now headed by Compass, a name so four-
square no novelist would dare invent it. With secondhand furni-
ture and federal money, police set up round-the-clock substations
in vacant apartments at three of the city's most deadly projects.
The 45 cops assigned to them work foot patrol, get to know the
law-abiding residents and sweep out the street dealers. They also
help pick up trash, combat graffiti and round up kids who play
hooky.

That mix of shoe leather and social work has made a difference. By the end of last year killings around the three projects
had dropped 74%. A dozen dead bodies per annum is still no
small problem. But if you don't happen to be one of them, it is
cause enough for celebration. Lately, the neighborhood even
sees its share of those spontaneous street parades that are defin-
ing outbreaks of civic life in New Orleans. What are people celebrating? Maybe just the return of their freedom to move around.

New Orleans is not alone. After years of depressing and implacable upswing, serious crime is retreating all around the U.S.
In the nine cities with a population of more than 1 million, the
decrease in violent crimes was 8% in 1994. Nationally, murders
fell 12% in the first six months of 1995, and serious crimes of all
kinds dropped 1% to 2%. The suburbs, long a growth area for felonies, posted declines between 4% and 5% last year in violent
crime.

What makes these numbers important, not just encouraging,
is that they extend what is plainly a sustained retreat from the
crack-fueled crime wave of the late 1980s. According to the FBI,
violent crimes started to decline in 1993. As always with crime,
an area of famously wiggly trend lines, the downward curve is not
to be found everywhere. Minneapolis, Minnesota, for instance, is
still puzzling over why in 1995 homicides climbed more than 56%
over the preceding year. Even with the downward trend, crime
rates remain bloodcurdlingly high, especially when compared to
the relatively peaceable kingdom of, say, 1965. (Murder victims
per 100,000 then: 5.1. In 1994: 9.) And there are widespread pre-

dictions that another tidal wave will break as soon as the milk-toothed children of the '90s crowd into their saw-toothed teens. Whoever called economics the dismal science must not have heard about criminology.

For all that, even the experts in bad behavior are intrigued. Something is happening here. The question is, Why? The lineup of contributing factors includes most of the usual suspects: a decline in the proportion of young males in the general population, the leveling off of crack cocaine use, a moderate unemployment rate and tougher sentencing that gets more felons off the street and keeps them off longer.

Certainly demographics is part of it. Very simply, there are fewer people in the most crime-prone category, which is males from the ages of 15 to 29. The crime spree that began in the 1960s was largely the work of baby boomers as they moved into those years. The same boomers are tipping into their 50s, an age when you're just right for fly fishing but not much good with a semiautomatic. The bad news, however, is that today's smaller cohort of teenagers is more prone to crime than its elders were at the same age. Among 14- to 17-year-olds, for instance, murder rates skyrocketed over the past decade.

The trade in crack cocaine also appears to have changed. Perhaps it has lost its cachet. "As with any drug epidemic, the attractiveness of the drug begins to wear off, partly because users see so many of their friends dead," says James Q. Wilson, the UCLA professor who is one of the nation's most prominent thinkers on crime. That's important, because crack was the great impetus to crime in the late 1980s as brash new dealers muscled in. Another theory is that the trade has simply stabilized into a "mature market," as they say in the business schools, with surviving distributors less likely to clash over territory.

As for prison populations, those have more than doubled in the past 15 years. Most criminologists believe that a relatively small population of repeat felons is responsible for a disproportionate share of crime. Lock away the most energetic thieves and killers, and you make a serious dent in their business. "Most prisoners *are* violent or repeat offenders," says William Bennett, the former Secretary of Education and drug czar. "Prisons *do* cut crime." Last week Bennett's Council on Crime in America, a commission he co-heads with Griffin Bell, who was Attorney General under Jimmy Carter, issued a report warning that violent crime is still higher than police records indicate because so much of it goes unreported. They urged even more aggressive jailings.

But time and again, the experts are also returning to an explanation they would have played down in the past: more effective policing strategies. It is respectable once again to believe that cops can have a real impact on crime rates, an opinion that has been seriously out of fashion among professional students of crime. For decades they held that crime was too deeply connected to underlying social causes, meaning everything from the state of the economy to the breakdown of the family. Such things are still assumed to play their part in producing crime. What has changed is the view that police are useful only to chase down bad guys after they strike.

All over the U.S., the decade of the '90s has seen a rapid reinvention of how the police do their jobs, especially in major cities. A change from squad cars to foot patrolling, a shift to "proactive" policing that seeks to dissolve problems such as open-air drug marts rather than just rack up arrests, the more frequent establishment of cross-agency task forces to target specific problems such as car theft, or drug crime—all are now commonplace. "This decline in crime rates is more than a demographic phenomenon," says Jeremy Travis, director of the National Institute of Justice, the research arm of the Justice Department. "Public policy can make a difference. Police can make a difference."

Exhibit A for supporters of the new policing is New York City, where major crime—murder, rape, robbery, auto theft, grand larceny, assault and burglary—is in something like statistical free fall, dropping 17.5% last year. Mayor Rudolph Giuliani and his police commissioner, William Bratton, both insist that the reason is their devotion to new ways of doing police business. John DiIulio Jr., a professor of politics and public affairs at Princeton University, says that since the mid-'80s top brass who embrace a similar shift in philosophy have risen to key positions in cities all around the country. "So now you're seeing better policing. Not miracles or panaceas, but *better policing.*"

To the extent that is true, police have had to pull themselves in two disparate directions—tougher and softer, as the COPS program in New Orleans illustrates. Tougher means more aggressive intervention. "If we see somebody we don't know, we ask them what they're doing there," says Compass. "If the story doesn't check out, we arrest them for trespassing. Now we don't see as many drug dealers around here." But at the same time, it has meant more neighborhood-friendly tactics, the foot patrolling and problem solving that form the loosely defined strategy called community policing. "We do neighborhood cleanups, counseling on child abuse, you name it," says Officer Djuana Adams. "We help the children with their homework, and they show up for treats when they get good grades."

New Orleans is also learning what other cities have discovered when they moved more officers away from the patrol-car policing that limited them to 911 emergency-response calls. The lesson: face-to-face contact between cops and the people they work among, with no windshield in between, helps to restore trust. For a city like New Orleans, which has recently seen some spectacular instances of police corruption, that is an invaluable side benefit. "I felt better almost as soon as the police moved in," says Brenda Holmes, who lives at Desire, the New Orleans housing project with the most poignant name. "They've given us our lives back."

The potential synergy between cops and residents works not only in big cities: Taylor, Texas, about 28 miles northeast of Austin, has just 13,300 people. But no place is too small for the drug trade. Five years ago, crack moved in among the cotton gins and railroad tracks, bringing with it assault, rape, car theft and murder. Crime got so bad that Mae Willie Turner, 79, and her sister, Gladys Hubbard, 73, could no longer sit at night on their front porch. "The place was infested," says Turner.

So they got off the porch and joined Turn Around Taylor, a community-action group designed to help locals take back their town. It was conceived by Herman Wrice, a Philadelphia management consultant who organizes citizen-led anticrime groups as part of a federal program. And the man who brought in Wrice and his ideas was Fred Stansbury, the police chief who arrived in Taylor in 1993, on an April day when a local teenager was killed in a gang fight. "We wanted a program where the community felt it had a proprietary interest," he says.

That's what they got. Most weeks Turner and Hubbard put on jackets with slogans such as UP WITH HOPE, DOWN WITH DOPE, and joined other demonstrators on streets where the heaviest dealing happened. Stansbury got the town council to designate "downtown" Taylor as a historic district, which meant a ban on the public consumption of alcohol. The group even persuaded the Texas National Guard to bulldoze 48 worn-out buildings near the railroad tracks that had become weekend squats for drug dealers and their customers, who used to come in by car and train. Taylor these days is more like it used to be. "I can sit on my porch anytime now," says Mae Willie Turner.

The single greatest imponderable in the crime debate is the role of gun control. Or decontrol: last week Texas became the 28th state to allow people to carry concealed weapons. The rationale is to discourage crime—supporters say felons will think twice about assaulting people who may be armed. Florida became the first state to pass such a law in 1987. Since then, more than 150,000 people there have applied for permits to pack a gun. But two recent studies suggest loopholes in the law have also allowed felons, ordinarily forbidden to carry a gun, to do so legally. On the other hand, gun homicides in Florida have declined 29% since the law was introduced. Michael McHargue of the Florida department of law enforcement shrugs, saying, "If you look at the overall statistical picture, we don't believe the law made any impression."

The effectiveness of gun laws that are stricter is no easier to compute. In the three cities with the most dramatic recent declines in homicide—New York, Kansas City and Houston—police have very aggressive strategies for separating felons from their firearms and stemming the flow of cheap, illegal handguns. Chicago is currently celebrating a decline in homicides from 930 in 1994 to 823 last year. Police think part of the reason might be that Illinois' new, stricter penalties for felonies involving a firearm have persuaded many gang members and drug dealers to leave the guns at home. "We'll arrest a whole crew and still find no guns," says Paul Jenkins, the Chicago police department's director of news affairs. But while the anecdotal evidence is suggestive, it is nothing like firm. "If we knew the reason for success, we'd do a lot more of it," says Jenkins. "We'd bottle it."

For now, keep the bottles uncorked. Talk to most experts in law enforcement, and they soon complain about the paucity of solid research to identify what works against crime. Norval Morris, a professor of law and criminology at the University of Chicago, compares the state of knowledge in his field to that in medicine earlier in the century, when doctors were commonly in the dark as to whether their treatments worked, or why. "Testing the consequences [for crime] of different drug policies, different housing practices, different police practices—it's very, very rarely done," he says.

In the 1988 presidential election, when rising crime was an issue, Willie Horton became the wanted-poster child who helped elect George Bush. In 1992 Bill Clinton neutralized the Republican advantage by positioning himself as a tough-on-crime Democrat who favored the death penalty and would put 100,000 new police officers on the streets. In an interview with *Time*, Clinton said last week that the country has embarked on a historic change: "What's happening now across America essentially closes the door on an era that began with the murder of Kitty Genovese 30 years ago." In that milestone episode of public indifference, Genovese, a young New Yorker, was murdered while dozens of people ignored her screams for help. "I think now we have ended both the isolation of the police from the community and the idea that the community doesn't have a responsibility to work with the police or with its neighbors."

Clinton's tough talk on crime helped him win back some of the Reagan Democrats who had fled the party. But with crime rates falling, the issue may lose some of the importance it had for voters two years ago. Though Americans still tell pollsters that crime is at the top of their concerns, that may change as lagging perceptions catch up to new realities. Meanwhile, the President sees the political advantage his. Though crime has hardly been as mentioned in the Republican primaries, the Clinton-Gore Re-Election Committee spent a surprising $2.4 million last summer on TV spots that ran in 24 states, touting the President's record on crime.

As the year goes on, expect Clinton to attack congressional Republicans for their attempt to rescind the 100,000-new-cops provision in his 1994 crime bill. In the White House version, municipalities get the money only if they use it to hire new officers and use them in community-policing programs. Republicans want to send that money instead in bloc grants to states to use as they see fit. Last month the President vetoed the appropriations bill that would have distributed his police money that way. "I don't tell all these folks how to deploy the police," said Clinton, "or what they should do all day. All I say is there has to be a community-policing strategy because that's by definition grass-roots reform, and we know that it works."

Or at least that it is part of what works. There may be a conjunction of half a dozen lucky developments that are holding crime in check right now. The trick will be to find the way to keep it all working. But for once, it is possible to suppose the trick is one we can manage.

THY NEIGHBOR'S RAP SHEET[2]

How Do You Know Whether a Killer Lives Next Door?

On New Year's Eve 1975, after an evening of taking LSD and watching cop shows on television, 15-year-old Raul Meza showed up at a convenience store near his house in Austin, Texas, armed with a deer rifle. Meza emptied the cash register, then marched the clerk, a 20-year-old college student named Derly Ramirez, into the walk-in freezer. Meza shot him in the back and left him for dead.

Ramirez recovered to testify against the man who wounded him. Meza received a twenty-year sentence, and served five years before getting out on parole.

On January 3, 1982, months after his release, 21-year-old Raul Meza abducted Kendra Page, a third-grader, as she rode her bicycle near her home in southeast Austin. Meza tortured, raped, and strangled the girl, then left her body behind a dumpster. Three days later, he surrendered to the police. Meza received 30 years for the killing.

While behind bars, Meza racked up demerits for various infractions, and four years were added to his sentence after guards found a knife in his cell. Meza came up for parole seven times, and each time it was denied.

By 1993, however, prison authorities could keep Meza no longer. Under Texas law, he had accumulated enough credit for good behavior to qualify automatically for release. The state freed him under mandatory supervision, a conditional release not

[2]Article by Tucker Carlson, a Bradley Fellow at The Heritage Foundation, from *Policy Review* 72:50-57 Ap '95. Copyright © 1995 by *Policy Review*. Reprinted with permission.

unlike parole that can be granted without the consent of the parole board.

No matter how notorious, most felons leave prison with little fanfare. They re-enter society quietly and soon become anonymous. Some begin new and honest lives. Many others, freed from supervision and accountable to no one, commit new crimes. Raul Meza might have regained his freedom in the same way, but he never got the chance. One hundred and forty miles from Meza's Huntsville prison cell, an Austin newspaper editor decided to make him famous.

In 15 years of covering crimes, Jerry White, the city editor of the *Austin American-Statesman*, had watched scores of criminals disappear from public view after sentencing. Most of them left prison years before their sentences expired, often to rob, rape, or kill again. "It became apparent," says White, "that even though these folks are sentenced and sent away, the story doesn't really end." White began compiling a list of inmates who were "fairly notorious" in Austin. Every few months, he called the department of corrections to ask when inmates on his list would be eligible for parole.

In June 1993, the department of corrections confirmed that Meza was due to be released soon. Using the state's Open Records Act, the newspaper petitioned Texas's attorney general and found where Meza planned to live. An article ran on the front page of the Sunday paper eight days before Meza's release. The headline read, 'Nothing's Going To Stop It': Killer of 8-Year-Old About to be Freed."

In a city of about 465,000 people, the story reached 240,000 homes and provoked an outpouring of media attention. Film crews greeted Meza as he walked out of the state prison and followed him for months. Publicity, mostly bad, seemed to trail him everywhere. Corrections officials moved him from town to town, but in each residents and local politicians protested his presence. Colin Amann, a Houston lawyer who represented the killer after his release, says angry citizens "kicked him in the butt from one end of Texas to the other."

For much of 1993, Texans kept on kicking. Over several months, he was shuttled between towns and cities all over the state. Of the 276 halfway houses that were asked to accept Meza, 271 refused. "Every town he went to," says Amann, "people were just screaming and yelling. Lots of small communities went out and bitched about it. A lot. And it happened every time they'd move him, they had the same outcry."

In August, the parole division placed Meza on his grandparents' farm, west of San Antonio. On August 31, local sheriffs charged Meza with "terroristic threatening" and disorderly conduct for bullying his elderly grandparents. A judge later dismissed the charges, but the incident made nearly every newspaper in Texas. At least 1,000 local residents signed a petition asking the state to move Meza again. The parole division sent him to Austin.

His new neighbors protested, held rallies, carried signs. A few moved away. The furor subsided a bit when the father of the murdered girl publicly called for citizens to give Meza the chance to start a new life. He moved into his mother's house and found a job. In the first 10 months of 1994, the *American-Statesman* ran more than 20 stories on Meza. In August 1994, he was arrested for violating the curfew provision of his parole, and he returned to the state prison in Huntsville.

At the time Meza was taken into custody, there were more than 116,000 parolees in Texas, 15,000 of whom had outstanding warrants for parole violations. Yet the governor's fugitive squad focused its energies on Meza, the most famous one. And while parolees in Texas routinely get three chances to break parole before being arrested, Meza was taken into custody after only one violation. His supporters cried foul. But the citizens of Texas were the better for it.

Meza needed all the attention he could get. As a group, violent sex offenders have an extraordinarily high rate of recidivism. In Texas, about one-third of convicted rapists are arrested for new crimes within two years of getting out on parole. Ordinarily, parole officers are not able to supervise sex offenders carefully. But because they learned from news reports where Meza lived, neighbors were able to keep their children out of his path. Relentless publicity forced a troubled parole system to work effectively. And information disseminated by the press helped to create thousands of civilian parole officers—watchful neighbors who kept an eye on him.

Publicity, however, is a blunt instrument, and others were unintentionally bludgeoned by Meza's fame. His relatives were humiliated. His victim's parents saw their tragedy replayed in the press. And Meza himself was hounded across the state. Nobody knows how such attention may have retarded his rehabilitation, but it may not matter. Despite the burdens imposed on him and his family—or, more likely, because of them—Meza did not kill another child while out of prison.

Even Meza's attorney, a self-described liberal, believes the publicity was worth the cost. "I think everybody should know when a parolee is coming to live in their neighborhood," says Colin Amann. "That's why crime is committed, because people don't know who the criminals are. Once they get out, let's let the entire world know where they are going to live. Let's let the community have some responsibility for keeping its thumb on them."

More and more communities are clamoring for that very responsibility. Meza's case illustrates what most people already sense: Citizens who know their neighbors will be safer than those who don't. Study after study has shown anonymity to be a factor in many crimes. Simply put, criminals are more apt to commit crimes in neighborhoods where they do not know the neighbors, and where the neighbors do not know one another. As James Q. Wilson and Richard Herrnstein explain in *Crime and Human Nature*, their expansive survey of criminology, "the more rapid the population turnover in an area, the higher the victimization rate, even after controlling for the racial and age composition."

Conversely, close-knit communities tend to be resistant to predatory crime. A criminal is less likely to commit crimes where the neighbors recognize him, particularly if they know that he has a criminal record.

Statistics explain why citizens have a vested interest in knowing who in their neighborhood has been convicted of serious offenses. Ex-cons commit a staggering amount of crime. As John DiIulio of Princeton University has pointed out, "within three years of sentencing, while still on probation, nearly half of all probationers are placed behind bars for a new crime or abscond." Nationally, recidivism for parolees is about the same as for probationers. DiIulio cites a revealing study of Florida convicts:

"Between 1987 and 1991, about 87 percent of the 147,000 felons released from Florida prisons were released early. Fully one-third of these parolees committed a new crime. At points in time when they would have been incarcerated had they not been released early, these parolees committed nearly 26,000 new crimes, including some 4,656 new crimes of violence—346 murders, 185 sexual assaults, 2,369 robberies, and 1,754 other violent offenses."

Not only are felons on supervised release dangerous, but there are a lot of them. In 1993, according to the Bureau of Justice Statistics, a total of 671,000 Americans were on parole or probation. There is considerable evidence that many parole and probation officers are responsible for far more offenders than they can possibly supervise, even those housed under one roof. An investigation in 1993 by the *Rocky Mountain News* found that one of every six convicted felons placed in Colorado halfway houses escaped. That year, the study found, 526 felons walked away from halfway houses and into the surrounding neighborhoods. Seven of the escapees were convicted murderers. "In most cases," the paper concluded, "no one looked for them."

Informed neighbors don't always just keep offenders from committing crimes; sometimes they can help ex-cons straighten out. Mike Elsworth got out of prison in Washington, D.C., for the last time on Halloween 1990, after serving two years for selling cocaine. Elsworth, who was paroled to the same part of town where he grew up, credits his neighbors for helping him keep his record clean since his release. Although he was shunned by at least one woman on his block, other "neighbors were supportive and understanding of me trying to do better once I got out. They knew I was looking for a job, and they would tell me about places that they knew were hiring, and some of them would tell me if I needed anything to come on by." Three months after his release, with the encouragement of his neighbors, Elsworth found a job.

Elsworth says his neighbors gave him the help and attention his parole officers did not. In two years, Elsworth reported to five different officers. "It was like, every three months I had a new one," he says, "I don't know why. They really had little or no concern about me as a person." Elsworth met with his parole officer for 10 to 15 minutes every few weeks. But he saw his neighbors every day, which ultimately, he says, made all the difference.

Of course, not all neighborhoods would take advantage of more information about felons. In some parts of cities, particularly in poor areas where citizens tend to live chaotic lives, neighbors often know who is on parole and don't care. Nor would giving neighbors the names and addresses of all newly released felons always benefit the felons themselves. Critics have long charged that releasing the names of parolees and probationers to the public would make it more difficult for convicted criminals to start successful new lives once they get out of prison. A federal judge recently struck down parts of "Megan's Law," a New Jersey statute requiring released sex offenders to tell their communities where they live. In his decision, Judge Nicholas Politan said the notification requirement amounted to a form of punishment, and cannot be added to penalties already in place before the law was passed in 1994. Requiring a convicted felon to notify his neighbors upon release, he wrote, would constitute a "lifelong albatross," and would ruin an ex-con's ability to "return to a normal, private, law-abiding life in the community." Judge Politan might be right. Ultimately, however, much of what would happen if the names of parolees were publicized is conjecture. As it stands, the identities of released criminals often remain shrouded in state and federal privacy laws. The Federal Privacy Act of 1974, for instance, generally bars authorities from divulging the names and addresses of parolees released from federal prisons. Most states, wary of civil-rights lawsuits brought by released felons, have adopted similar laws. While the intent of such statutes may be noble, their effect has sometimes been devastating.

Last summer, the residents of Red Hook, a small town in upstate New York, paid the price for having an unknown felon in their midst. In June, Richard Moran, a lifelong criminal from the Bronx, was released from Rikers Island, where he had spent the previous three months on a parole violation, and placed in Red Hook's only homeless shelter. No one knew his criminal record. No one was watching.

Had Moran's record become public, Tommy McCauliff, a 29-year-old with cerebral palsy, might still be alive. On a Sunday afternoon in July, McCauliff emerged from his apartment, staggered across the street, and bled to death on the sidewalk from a knife wound in his back.

Police picked up Moran and charged him with second-degree murder. He was later convicted.

By the time he came to Red Hook, Moran had spent close to half of his 43 years behind bars. First arrested in New York City for armed robbery in 1969, he went on to amass 26 different criminal charges, including several violent felonies. Within days of being released, Moran made his way to Shelter Plus, a state-financed boarding house for vagrants in Red Hook, 90 miles north. Under circumstances that are still not clear, he met Tommy McCauliff.

When an inmate with two or more convictions is released from a state prison in New York, within 48 hours corrections officials must notify the police in the town to which he is headed. Rikers Island, however, is not a state prison, but a jail run by New York City. Authorities there were not required to notify police in Red Hook that Moran was on his way to their town. And they didn't.

The state's department of social services in nearby Poughkeepsie was the only agency that knew about Moran's arrival in Red Hook, and New York's confidentiality laws require social workers to keep secret the criminal histories of their clients.

"Anything in our records is confidential," says John Battistoni, the county's commissioner of social services. "Parolees just come in like anyone else. If they're without a place to go, we're required to give them shelter." Only a court order, he says, can force the department to divulge the names of the parolees it places in homeless shelters. A call from the local police department will not suffice. For employees who break confidentiality rules, says Battistoni, "the penalties could be severe. You'd be subjecting yourself and your county to all sorts of suits. It's tough stuff."

All things considered, says Battistoni, he is not bothered by the secrecy. "I suppose people shouldn't be branded," he offers. "People are saying they'd like to know if a criminal is placed in their neighborhood. I often wonder what they would do with the information if they had it. Put a 24-hour tail on the guy?"

Lisa Murray has no doubt what she would do with such information. "I would keep an eye on that person," she says, "and I would know if that person was near my child, if it was a rapist or a child molester, to get my kid away." Murray is one of five Red Hook women who formed a group called Concerned Citizens for a Safe Community after McCauliff's death. The group advocates changing the confidentiality laws they believe were partly responsible for the killing.

Murray points out that Richard Moran is not the only criminal to move into the homeless shelter without the town's knowledge. Since McCauliff's death, police have arrested two other residents of Shelter Plus for selling drugs. "Whenever somebody gets a DWI or commits a robbery, it's in the paper before they're even convicted of the crime," she says. "So why not have a criminal who's already been convicted of a crime and released from prison be put in the paper saying where he's going to live?"

A county legislator named Woody Klose quickly sponsored a resolution requiring local police to be notified whenever felons are placed in homeless shelters. Steve Saland, a state senator, sponsored a bill that would force corrections officials to notify towns whenever a parolee is about to be released into their midst. Unlike the statute in place, the new law would apply to jails as well as state prisons. It would require authorities to notify the mayor and the chief of police of the town to which the parolee is headed, as well as officials in the town where the crime was committed. The written statement would include the ex-con's physical description, his known aliases, and his criminal record. It would also contain his new home address. Towns would have to post the information in a public place, such as a bulletin board in city hall, in post offices, or in advertisements in local newspapers. Released offenders would be required to report to local authorities for a period of 10 years each time they moved to a new address in New York.

Saland's notification law would apply only to paroled sex criminals, repeat violent offenders, and those convicted of three or more felonies. Saland says the law would not prevent parolees from committing new crimes. But it might help neighbors to protect themselves from released criminals. "All you can do is provide notice," he says. After that, "it's up to the community."

Tommy McCauliff's death prompted New York politicians to take a new look at an old debate. For years, lawmakers have tried to balance the requirements of public safety with a belief that stigmatizing released felons makes rehabilitating them more difficult. Many states have compromised by requiring parolees and convicted criminals to register their addresses with law-enforcement officials, but not with neighbors or community groups. States that do provide for community notification when a felon is released nearly always limit the notification to cases involving sex offenders.

Most states that have such laws leave their application to the discretion of law enforcement officers. Often police departments get to decide which sex offenders constitute a threat to their neighbors. Although the state of Washington allows police to release photographs of and information about convicted sex offenders to community groups, and news outlets, the law is not always used. In the first 10 months of 1994, for instance, county police in Spokane notified the public only once of a paroled sex offender, though several were released into the area. Carol Dorris, who follows crime legislation for the National Victim's Center, says it is not unusual to see effective laws passed, then ignored. "It's fine to put in statutes and legislate something," she says, "but to enforce them is a lot harder to do."

Nevertheless, recent developments show that concerned citizens have several outlets for civic action:

Legislative Action. The inability of probation officers to effectively track offenders argues for comprehensive notification laws—let the community provide the surveillance that the state cannot or will not. So far, such laws exist only in theory. For fear of destroying an ex-con's chances of success after release, no state has passed laws that would give the public the names and addresses of all parolees and probationers.

Louisiana, however, has taken the lead in warning communities about released sex offenders. In 1992, the legislature passed two laws that ensure sex offenders will never again live anonymously in Louisiana. Or, as a later revision to the laws put it, "Persons found to have committed a sex offense have a reduced expectation of privacy." In fact, a person convicted of one of the state's 18 sex offenses can expect practically no privacy at all.

The two laws and their amendments are vast in scope. No later than 10 days before a sex offender gets out of prison, corrections officials must send letters warning of his impending release to his victims, witnesses who testified against him, and the sheriff of the parish (county) to which he is going. Once he gets out, a sex offender must register with the sheriff and provide his fingerprints, his photograph, his social-security number, and any aliases he has used. The ex-con must also give the sheriff a description of his offense, including the date and place he committed it, and his home address. Offenders who move within the state of Louisiana have 10 days to re-register. The process continues for 10 years after their release.

If his victim was a juvenile at the time of the offense, the offender must notify his neighbors as well. Twice within his first month out of prison, he must purchase an advertisement in his local newspaper. The ads must reveal his name, his address, and his offense. Descriptions of the crimes must be written in language ordinary citizens can understand; statute numbers do not suffice. To verify that it meets these specifications, the ad must pass muster with a parole officer.

One such classified advertisement, which appeared in the *New Orleans Times-Picayune* on May 8, 1994, is typical of the genre. "John Jones of 701 Teche St.," it said, "was convicted of a Sex Offense, Simple Rape." Another, on June 10, 1994, advertised, "I, Jim Davis, was convicted of molestation of a juvenile." . . . Other ads placed in the paper in June mentioned carnal knowledge, sexual battery, and indecent behavior with a juvenile.

Once he has notified the larger community of his crime, an offender must tell his neighbors about it. The parolee must send letters or postcards with the same information—name, address, and offense—to every house within three blocks of his home. In cities, this usually means 36 square blocks and hundreds of houses. A parolee who lives in a rural area must send letters to everyone within a one-mile radius of his house.

Finally, a sex offender whose victim was under 18 must contact the superintendent of the public-school district in his parish, as well as the principals of any private or parochial schools in the area.

If it chooses, a parole board also "may order any other form of notice which it deems appropriate, including but not limited to signs, handbills, bumper stickers, or clothing labeled to that effect." All of the expenses involved in the notification, such as stamps, envelopes, and advertising fees—not to mention any specially-labeled clothing the parole board may require—must be borne by the parolee. If at any time he fails to meet any requirement, an offender may be returned to prison.

Citizen Journalists. When John Roger, president of the Bayview Civic League in Norfolk, Virginia, asked the local police department to release the names of parolees who had moved into his neighborhood, it refused. Undeterred, Roger sought information at the other end of the criminal justice system: arrestees.

Unlike the addresses of released felons, arrest records are publicly available from the police department. Every month, the league's newsletter, *Bayview Bylines*, publishes the name, race, and home address of each person taken into custody by the police within the boundaries of the Bayview neighborhood. Periodically, in a feature called "Pervert Alert," Roger also provides descriptions of flashers, peeping Toms, and other unsavory characters seen in the area. To pay for printing, local merchants buy advertising space in the newsletter. "Want to know why we do it?" he asks. "It's simple. We live here. We believe our members have a right to know what's going on."

Though he prints only 4,000 copies of the newsletters, Roger is confident they reach many more people. Residents read it, he says, not only out of a fear of crime, but to "find if somebody they know has been arrested." The publicity can have consequences. Landlords, says Roger, scan the names of arrestees. "If it happens to be one of their tenants, they get rid of him."

Although it remains difficult in most states to learn the whereabouts of parolees, there are other ways citizens can gather information on potentially dangerous criminals. In July 1994, John Johansen, a financial consultant in Arlington, Virginia, published the first issue of *Crime Prevention Bulletin*, a quarterly newspaper with a circulation of 30,000. Police departments in Washington, D. C., and suburban Maryland and Virginia cooperated with Johansen, giving him the photographs and last known addresses of fugitives in the area. Johansen printed the mug shots, some beneath headlines like "Wanted for Murder." The papers were distributed throughout the area by members of neighborhood organizations.

The *Bulletin* was an instant success. In many cases, fugitives were still living in the same areas, even at the same addresses, amid neighbors who had no idea they were wanted by the law. Local police did not have the resources to track down each of the fugitives. But they could respond to tips provided by citizens who recognized their neighbors in the *Bulletin*. In its first six months, police credited Johansen's newspaper with the arrests of 15 fugitives in Washington alone. Six of them were suspected murderers.

Do-It-Yourself Advertising. Sanford "Sandy" Krasnoff, the president of Victims and Citizens Against Crime, in Louisiana, says his group devotes much of its energy to making certain the state's sex-crimes laws achieve their desired effect. Every Saturday morning, the flamboyant Krasnoff, who at various times in his career has been a New Orleans cop, a lawyer, and a manager of professional prize fighters, hosts a radio show called "Crime Watch." Each week, during three hours of air-time donated by the station, Krasnoff announces the names, addresses, and crimes of all sex offenders released on parole or probation in Louisiana in the previous week. Krasnoff gets the information directly from the parole and pardons board.

Krasnoff's group also monitors offenders after their release. A volunteer, whom Krasnoff refers to as "the sex lady," scans newspapers for advertisements placed by parolees under the new law. When he saw that some of the ads were "coming out in mumbo-jumbo, referring to act numbers and statutes instead of telling people exactly what they were charged with," Krasnoff wrote a letter to the department of corrections, which promptly instructed parole officers to reject such ads.

According to William T. Price, the deputy director of the state's adult probation and parole division, the state's new sex-offender laws have not prompted violence from the public. In a few cases, people moved upon learning that a child molester had come to their neighborhood. But, he says, nobody has yet thrown a fire bomb.

Price does worry that the laws may be too broad, covering not only child molestation and forcible rape, but also non-predatory crimes like bigamy. "If you can attach the concept of sex to it," says Price, a crime probably falls under the rubric of the new laws.

For all its willingness to publicize the names and addresses of sex offenders, the state of Louisiana still guards information about other parolees carefully. Apart from sex criminals, the state's probation and parole division refuses to give out the home addresses of the convicts it supervises. The concern, says Price, is that some people, such as bill collectors, could put the information to unwholesome purposes. "We don't want to get into that business," he says.

In the fall of 1994, residents of Warwick, Rhode Island, a Providence suburb, were desperate to publicize the whereabouts of a man named Craig Price. Five years before, Price had admitted stabbing to death four of his Warwick neighbors. Because he was technically a juvenile when he committed the murders, he was sentenced to a juvenile detention center until age 21. Incensed by Price's crime, a Warwick police captain named Kevin Collins organized citizens to fight his release. "This guy had butchered four people," says Collins, "knowing that when he gets out at 21, he can go out and obtain a gun, [or] work in a day-care center."

Collins decided to keep Craig Price from ever becoming anonymous. He recounted Price's story on radio and television shows. He sent press releases to papers around the country. When he heard that Price planned to move to Florida upon release, Collins hired an airplane to tow a sign over Miami Beach. The banner read, "Killer of 4 Craig Price Moving Here? No Police

Record!" Similar messages floated over Chicago and beaches in Los Angeles and New Jersey.

Once Price is released, Collins says, he will not be able to tell the public where the killer lives. "Once he gets out there—like if he moves into your neighborhood," says Collins, "if I went around there knocking on doors, I think they're going to come after me on a civil-rights violation." Collins says the memory of the man's crimes may be enough to keep Price from killing again in Rhode Island. "Hey, my attitude is, he deserves to be a prisoner of public opinion."

Exercising the Right to Know. Although no Rhode Island statute would prevent Collins from publicizing Craig Price's address once the killer is released, doing so would be unwise. As a police officer, Collins could wind up in federal court under Title VII of the United States Code. Passed in 1964 as part of Lyndon Johnson's civil-rights legislation, the law allows individuals to bring civil action against government officials who conspire to deprive them of rights guaranteed under the Constitution. Courts have interpreted the law liberally, and it is conceivable that Collins could be found to have violated Price's right to privacy, a protection some judges believe emanates from the Fourth Amendment.

The state's privacy act prohibits government officials from releasing a parolee's medical records, or information about his drug or alcohol treatment. But no regulations prohibit the state from giving out his home address to citizens who ask. The privacy law does not bind Rhode Islanders who do not work for the government. Says James Jerue, chairman of the state's parole board, if Craig Price were released on parole in Rhode Island, any citizen could find out where he lived. Not that Jerue thinks citizens would try to learn. "It has never happened," he says. "No one has ever asked for a home address."

Citizens have a right to know when potentially dangerous criminals are released into their neighborhoods. But they also have an obligation to make the effort required to find the information. And there are many ways to get it.

• In places like Rhode Island, citizens can simply ask the state for the names and addresses of parolees.

• In states with strict privacy laws, such as New York, citizens can lobby the legislature for legal reform.

• Individuals can ask newspapers to publish the results of every parole hearing in the state, as well as the names of every person arrested and convicted for a serious crime. Once such information becomes public, it can be spread to a wider audience on community bulletin boards and computer services.

• Citizens' groups can apply political pressure to police departments to release the names and addresses of those arrested and of those being released from prison into the area.

• No citizens' group should underestimate the power of a well-placed news story to make police departments more accommodating to its requests. If public scrutiny helps to keep criminals honest, it can have the same effect on public officials. More than anything, concerned citizens must be willing to spend time and energy gathering information on known criminals. Which means they must be nosy. An informed community is not necessarily the most private, but it will be the safest.

CRIME AND PUNISHMENT[3]

It sometimes takes outrages to change the law, and extreme cases are fueling a campaign to extend prison terms. Darnell Collins was paroled last year in New Jersey after serving half of a 20-year robbery sentence. Last week he killed seven people in a five-day horror spree. In Oklahoma, state Judge Gary Lumpkin recalls his shock while hearing the appeal of an armed robber sentenced 14 months earlier to a 10-year term. The man, already released, was in court listening. Says James Wootton of the Washington-based Safe Streets Alliance: "The justice system allows violent criminals out too easily, and the public wants that changed."

With crime the runaway leader among American's worries, politicians are finding themselves in a bind. Fearful constituents demand a crackdown, but they also want tax cuts and basic services. Factor in the need to respect convicts' legal rights and a crisis is at hand. "States are realizing that they cannot afford to

[3]Article by Ted Gest with Jennifer Seter, Dorian Friedman, and Kevin Whitelaw from *U.S. News & World Report* 119/1:24-6 Jl 3, '95. Copyright © July 3, 1995, U.S. News & World Report. Reprinted with permission.

satisfy the public cries for vengeance," says Steven Donziger of the private National Criminal Justice Commission, who spoke last week at a "summit" on prison construction convened in Washington by architects and state prison directors.

Oklahoma is a case in point. Its prisons are overflowing . . . , but Republican Frank Keating won the governorship last year partly on a pledge to get even tougher. The Legislature ended its session in late May squabbling over how to pay for prison expansion. Then the governor faced a court hearing over housing inmates in two turn-of-the-century cellblocks a judge had declared unfit. Keating, who recently told prison wardens that their institutions house "slimeballs," was stymied. Admitting his action was "not sound corrections policy," he declared a state of emergency and authorized early releases of about 500 convicts. Noting that prisons had received larger increases than other agencies, state Sen. Cal Hobson observed: "It's getting more and more difficult to find enough money for every state need."

Tough-talking officials in state after state are being forced to reconcile competing interests. In Michigan, which may soon run out of empty prison beds, Gov. John Engler said last week that "all of us look at the futility of having to spend money on prisons, but we recognize the public necessity." A state panel will consider an overhaul of sentencing laws. In New York, legislative leaders agreed with Gov. George Pataki in early June on a plan to ease a crowding crisis by boosting penalties for violent criminals while reducing those for many sentenced under tough 1970s-era antidrug laws. Eventually, California may be faced with what the Rand Corp. estimates will be $5.5 billion in added annual costs—$300 per taxpayer—to meet the "three strikes and you're out" law that gives life terms to repeat offenders.

The high cost of punishment has prompted some politicians to focus on the flashier issue of prison perks. Critics portray inmates munching steak dinners, dialing up premium cable-television channels and exercising on fancy equipment. "Stop building prisons like Holiday Inns" is a mantra in recent focus groups by GOP pollster Frank Luntz, says the firm's Mark Allen.

Never mind that the typical prison is noisy, dirty and dangerous. Lawmakers in Washington and several states want to ban everything from air conditioning to hot plates in cells. Alabama and Arizona have reinstituted chain gangs; other states may join them and start caning as well. "There is a spirit of meanness, selfishness and punitiveness that seems to have no bounds," says Alvin Bronstein of the American Civil Liberties Union's National Prison Project.

Recently, the focus has shifted to hard labor. Alabama Sen. Richard Shelby says states wanting federal prison-building aid should require inmates to work 48 hours a week (he issued a cartoon of a striped-uniform inmate breaking rocks). House Speaker Newt Gingrich backs an inmate work regime. "We need to fundamentally overhaul the prison system," he says. Pollster Allen reports the issue has "caught on fire" in focus groups.

However the perks-and-work controversy plays out, the hard decision making will turn on cost-effectiveness. No one opposes punishment, but how much is enough? Incarceration has had only a limited impact on crime. While inmate populations jumped fourfold in the past two decades, violent-crime rates varied erratically. "It doesn't take an Einstein to tell you if prison were the answer, crime should have dropped," says Tim Matthews of the American Probation and Parole Association. Other experts estimate that putting more criminals behind bars may have helped avert between 5 and 15 percent more violent crimes.

Many states are building away, ignoring the fact that "everybody and his mother don't need to be in prison," says John DiIulio of Washington's Brookings Institution. He says some offenders such as nonviolent drug users, "are being put in the most expensive form of imprisonment when they don't need that kind of oversight." The National Council on Crime and Delinquency forecast at last week's summit that the nation's prisoner rolls might exceed 1.6 million by 2001 if states require inmates to serve 85 percent of their terms, a goal of the new federal crime law.

Depending on the budget war's outcome, Congress may offer several billion dollars to help states open prisons for violent convicts. For now, states are trying a variety of approaches:

• **Building up.** Texas has launched an unprecedented construction boom to raise prison capacity from 38,000 in 1987 to a projected 150,000 by 1997. Many prisoners are housed in spartan dormitory-style structure. So far, Texans are footing the $4.5 billion bill in the next two years—a burden that may be difficult to sustain. Carl Reynolds of the state Board of Criminal Justice warns Texas may have to resort to "built-in gimmicks at the back end" that permit early releases. In Florida, where legislators recently enacted sentencing laws that could double the prison population to 120,000 by 2002, funding will "come directly from education, health and social services," predicts Brian Berkowitz of a state corrections panel.

• **Ending parole.** "People were disgusted with the dishonesty and leniency of the system," says Virginia Gov. George Allen. Last year, legislators ended parole and more than doubled expected prison time for many first-time violent offenders. But they gave Allen only one-fourth of what he sought for construction. Critics like state Sen. Joseph Gartlan charge that Allen wants to spend too much on building and not enough on prevention.

A similar scenario may unfold in Pennsylvania, where a paroled killer is accused of murdering a New Jersey police officer. Critics seek to end parole for the violent regardless of cost. "Pennsylvania wants to spend that money," says state Sen. Mike Fisher.

• **Truth in sentencing.** New North Carolina guidelines direct judges to sentence defendants for periods they actually will serve. The penalties are tied to prison capacity so prisons do not overflow. The system, which began last October, has produced "reverse sticker shock," says Robin Lubitz of the state Sentencing Commission. "The public is used to hearing 20 to 40 years; now it's two to four years." Some terms are higher. Second-degree murderers, for example, will serve about 14 years, compared with 7.6 under the old system. But the percentage of felons going to prison has dropped from 47 to 32, with lesser offenders getting nonprison penalties.

• **Lesser measures.** The drive to punish the violent more harshly has intensified a search for "intermediate sanctions" for those criminals who don't need high security. Fewer than 1 in 5 persons serving a sentence are in federal or state prisons. The rest—some 4,000,000—are on probation or parole, or serving short stints in local jails. The public may back alternatives more than some politicians think: A new *U.S. News* survey found that when asked which is more important in stopping crime, Americans choose prevention over punishment, 45 to 38 percent.

Perhaps the fastest-growing alternative to prison is "drug courts" that send mostly first-time offenders to supervised treatment. Attorney General Janet Reno champions the idea based on a tribunal in Dade, her home county in Florida. Even though that model has been criticized for releasing too many violent criminals, the Clinton administration persuaded Congress to help other areas create drug courts. Already, 37 have been set up, and the Justice Department reports that more than 130 other places have applied for aid.

Military-style boot camps also are multiplying as an alternative to long prison terms. At least 35 states run such facilities, where convicts spend up to six months in a strict regimen of physical exercise and work. Graduates commit new crimes at about the same rate as do those who went to prison, but camps that add education or drug treatment show promise of reducing recidivism, says criminologist Doris MacKenzie of the University of Maryland.

Intensive probation is the watchword in other places. Wisconsin is trying "neighborhood supervision." Instead of managing caseloads spread over a huge area, officers are assigned to small areas where they try to befriend residents and, officials hope, have a better chance of keeping track of convicts.

Cost Cutting

Many of the alternatives don't necessarily save much money, but one that does is "day reporting," pioneered in Massachusetts and replicated in two dozen other states. Parolees check in 365 days a year en route to work or to getting counseling and drug and alcohol testing. Annual costs are $7,000 to $12,000 per convict, far below the average $19,000 cost of imprisonment nationally. Elsewhere, as many as 100,000 convicts are required to have their whereabouts tracked with devices attached to their bodies. As popular as electronic monitoring is, it still affects a minuscule fraction of probationers.

The punishment battle is being waged state by state, but forces in Washington are maneuvering to influence the outcome. The 1994 federal anticrime law gives states that have adopted "truth in sentencing" rules preference when prison-building money is handed out if convicts are required to serve 85 percent of their sentences. Crime-victim advocates fear that the law's tough-minded purpose will be undermined by a clause soon to be implemented by the Clinton administration that calls on states to develop plans for nonprison penalties. The Justice Department denies any laxity: "There is a consensus among Democrats and Republicans to put predatory offenders behind bars," says Assistant Attorney General Laurie Robinson. But House Republicans repealed the provision as part of the Contract With America. The Senate has yet to act.

Congressional Republicans also want to curb lawsuits filed by watchdog groups challenging prison conditions. The House approved a measure that would void cases on file in several dozen states after critics charged that judges were micromanaging institutions. The bill could have a "devastating impact" on cases like the one that prompted Oklahoma's Keating to order early releases, says the ACLU's Edward Koren. It's not clear whether the Supreme Court would uphold such a law under the Constitution's ban on "cruel and unusual punishment," but the court last week issued a 5-to-4 ruling that makes it harder for inmates to challenge disciplinary measures.

The struggle over crime and punishment in America will be fought in state capitals, where policy makers will be forced to bust budgets or else back away from get-tough promises. A new report from a national panel of governors' policy aides advises a careful study of justice trade-offs before an infamous crime inflames public passions. The lesson "may not be satisfying for governors," warns panel director Eric Brenner, but "crime is a fact of life today, and it will not be eliminated in four years. Skepticism over easy answers is usually warranted."

STUDENT SERVICE PROJECTS PREVENT CRIME[4]

There is an increasing perception that young people are angry, irredeemable, and responsible for the growing violence problem. Yet, too often, society waits until young people become a problem before helping them. The fact is, while the teen violence rate has risen in recent years, teens are also the group most likely to be victimized by crime.

By focusing our public policy and education decisions on the violent crimes young people commit, we ignore two critical pieces

[4]Article by Erin Donovan from *The Education Digest*, September 1995, 61/1:23-5. Copyright © 1995 by *The Education Digest*, Ann Arbor, Michigan. Reprinted with permission.

of the solution to youth violence. Young people need (1) educational programs that teach them how to be safe and (2) programs that help them find opportunities to apply this life-saving information to their schools and communities. Service learning provides both these understandings, as well as the positive recognition, outlet for energy, meaningful work, and bonds to the community that help young people become responsible citizens.

Teens offer an enormous pool of untapped energy, talent, and enthusiasm. The vast majority hope for a better life and seek opportunities to participate in and serve the larger society. They cry out for recognition and a sense of belonging. When such support is not found, the cry too often takes the form of a deviant act.

By providing teens with service projects that help them become part of the crime-prevention solution, schools and communities create climates that send them a positive message, claiming them as valuable community members. The projects offer them opportunities to develop self-esteem; critical thinking, problem solving, communication, leadership, and citizenship skills; and the confidence that they can play an important role in making their schools and neighborhoods safe. Teenagers with a strong sense of self-esteem who have a stake in their communities are less likely to become involved in prevalent teen crimes.

For young people on the fringe, being asked to contribute can become the first step toward positive, healthy engagement with their schools and communities. Adults who may have been quick to blame young people see them doing something positive and rethinking their attitudes. Having demonstrated their potential to society, these young people feel more valued, and they become less prone to crime. They have a clearer sense of purpose, and they have formed bonds that help protect them from delinquency. We owe them this opportunity. Their lives depend on it.

From its beginning, the Teens, Crime, and Community (TCC) program, a nationally recognized crime prevention and service-learning program, has combined community service with crime-prevention education to reduce high teen-victimization rates. It is critical for effective citizenship and for fighting crime that young people believe they can control the circumstances of their lives, protect themselves, and better their communities.

The classroom is a natural environment in which to introduce and apply the concept of community service to reduce local crime problems. Whenever problems are daunting, pulling together as a class to solve them as a mutual concern greatly increases students' confidence and their chance for success.

While students nearly always report that they have learned a great deal from the TCC curriculum alone, the service projects reinforce and extend that learning. They help students see the practical value of their instruction and the way it results in meaningful action against crime. And the programs help strengthen contacts with community resource persons and agencies. Those students who have shown an interest in the subject matter addressed by a particular resource person may want to develop that interest further by designing a project that addresses that issue or assists that person's organization, for example.

The TCC found four important factors that define successful service projects and contribute to their success:

1. Service projects must be teen designed and teen led. Though students work with adult mentors, for maximum benefit, it is critical for students to be responsible for carrying out their projects. One of the main purposes of service projects is to help teens understand their capacity as resources to prevent crime. Teens challenged to make changes and given the skills and freedom to plan and carry out service projects are more successful at translating classroom knowledge into effective community action.

2. Service projects must result in real change. Changes teens can effect in the community are as important as teen attitudes and the connection they feel to their communities. The term *service project* is used for a reason—to spur teens to demonstrate how they can change their environment. The change could be raising the school's or community's awareness of crime and crime-prevention issues, educating through specific crime-prevention messages, or advocating or fund-raising for crime-prevention or victim-assistance programs.

3. Service projects must be completed in one semester. Projects are most effective and instructive when they can be planned and executed in one semester. This allows students to see projects through to completion and helps ensure that the project ideas and planning process remain manageable. Students are most eager to act on information they have just learned. (This does not rule out projects that extend beyond the semester. Motivated students should always be encouraged to continue to pursue community service.)

4. Service projects must be based on local problems. Since teens need to connect to the community and see the immediate relevance of their classwork, a grounding in the local situation—the needs of the school or neighborhood—is necessary. In addition, no single project or particular crime-prevention strategy fits every situation. Students must assess the local situation and select project topics and approaches that best fit those circumstances. In one community, the issue might be drug abuse; in another, drunk driving; in yet another, assault or vandalism. Community education efforts, physical improvement projects, cross-age teaching programs, or mediation all might be used to address local needs.

The TCC experience with crime-prevention service projects has been very positive. Urban, rural, and suburban young people have been highly creative in their approaches. In Hibbing and Chisolm, Minnesota, the TCC program is a partnership between the schools and the regional corrections office. . . . [In 1995] students worked with the local radio station to create public service announcements aimed at preventing community crime. Each week, students selected a different crime-prevention message from the TCC textbook. For example, after completing the conflict management chapter, they created an announcement that encourages people to think of as many options as possible when faced with a conflict.

In North Charleston, South Carolina, TCC students have been working with local nurseries and hardware stores on a school beautification project. The program has been so successful that participants decided to expand with new projects, including cross-age teaching and creation of a TCC gospel choir. The choir consists of TCC students who visit the local elementary schools. Through their music, they provide crime-prevention messages and speak to students about ways the TCC has influenced their lives. They also encourage the elementary children to attend TCC classes when they get to middle school.

In Boston, TCC students were alarmed by the number of billboards in their community that advertised alcohol. They lobbied to have the billboards removed and other billboards simultaneously purchased that provide crime-prevention and healthful behavior messages.

Service projects can be as simple as a classroom crime-prevention poster or as ambitious as a neighborhood cleanup. What matters is the people who do them, and those who benefit—youth and their communities.

SUE THE GOVERNMENT[5]

For thirty years we have watched as violent crime has escalated to frightening levels and allowed "the crime issue" to become a mirror of other anxieties—about race, values, class, anything but the violence itself. Both right and left have engaged in a variety of self-serving denials. Liberals have demanded more and more "rights," while scanting the right to be secure from violence. Conservatives have attacked "command-and-control" regulation from the center, but when it comes to crime, they've championed the crudest law-and-order palliatives.

Maybe there's another way. A better approach to crime would both take it seriously as the pre-eminent social problem and take stock of what we've learned in other areas of government. If reducing violence is a serious goal, we should think about ensuring that the states have financial incentives to make progress toward it. Put another way, think of security from violence as a personal right—not a special right for minorities and the poor, enforced by baffled federal judges improvising injunctions through rounds of "public law litigation." Make it a serious right of the kind beloved by middle-class plaintiffs: a claim for individual, financial damage payments from government for defaulting on its obligation to protect citizens from violent crime.

Is this a crazy suggestion? It draws, in fact, on one of the oldest traditions in the Anglo-American system of criminal justice. Crime control, in this tradition, is a community responsibility and when the community defaults, it must answer to the victims. A key echo of this medieval tradition lived on in the statute books of many American states until quite recently—in fact, until the

[5]Article by Jeremy A. Rabkin, a teacher at Cornell University, from *New Republic*, 212:19 My 8 '95. Copyright © 1995 by *The New Republic*. Reprinted with permission.

outset of the crime wave that began to soar during the 1960s. It's a tradition perfectly suited to the crime problem of the present day.

The medieval version of this approach was formalized with the Statute of Winchester, issued during the reign of King Edward I in 1285. Local communities had long been responsible for launching a "hue and cry" to hunt down perpetrators of violent crime. By the thirteenth century, many localities seemed to be shirking this duty, closing inquiries with oaths by the neighbors that they knew nothing about the criminals. So the Statute of Winchester obligated the local residents to pay damages to the victims of violent crime, if they couldn't catch the villains within forty days—"so that henceforth, for fear of the Pain more than for fear of any Oath, they shall not spare any, nor conceal any Felonies." Decades later, this measure was reaffirmed, along with the due process guarantees of Magna Carta, as a fundamental safeguard for the personal security of English subjects.

In the early eighteenth century, Parliament enacted a more focused measure, making cities and counties responsible for reimbursing damages perpetrated by a "riot" (defined as a "tumultuous gathering for illegal purposes" of three or more persons). Parliament re-enacted this measure in slightly modified form in the early nineteenth century and in this form it passed into the statutes of a number of American states. In the wake of the draft riots of 1863, New York City was thus faced with 1,000 separate lawsuits demanding compensation for damage the authorities had failed to prevent. A state appeals court eventually affirmed the New York Riot Act as an entirely constitutional device; it described the measure as an appropriate means to "make good at public expense" the losses suffered "by acts of lawless violence . . . which it is the general duty of the government to prevent."

The idea caught on. In 1871 the U.S. House of Representatives, citing the New York practice, voted for a package of federal measures that would have imposed financial liability on any locality that failed to prevent or suppress racial violence. Sponsors of the measure predicted such damage awards might well require localities to impose special new taxes; such financial pressures, they said, would soon force Southern property holders to help suppress "outrages of Ku Kluxery." This federal measure was ultimately defeated in the Senate. But the New York state riot law and similar laws in other states remained in force well into this century. In the late nineteenth century, a Pennsylvania court credited a parallel measure with having forced substantial improvements in crime control in Philadelphia.

More recently, however, most states have given up on the notion that cities should be held accountable for suppressing riots. New York state suspended its statute during World War II, ostensibly on the grounds that police resources might be needed for "national defense" measures during the wartime "emergency." The state legislature then cited the "threat of atomic and radiological warfare" as grounds for extending the suspension during the 1950s and '60s. Those who sought compensation from the city for damage from the race riots of 1943 and 1964 were denied judicial relief on this ground. Eventually, the state legislature acknowledged the new policy by repealing the old law outright in 1971. By that time, Louisiana, Illinois, California, and other states—evidently in response to race riots of the 1960s—had repealed their parallel measures. Cities could no longer accept responsibility for suppressing mob rule.

At the same time, violence began a steady rise—murder rates doubling in many cities, rates of armed assault and rape increasing at still higher rates in the 1960s and '70s. Of course, the denial of municipal responsibility for mob or gang crime wasn't the cause. But it was symptomatic of the response: cities overwhelmed with violence essentially shrugged their shoulders and hoped the frightening trends of that era would eventually subside. They did not.

What happened instead was that the costs of crime were privatized. Rather than a public obligation, for which the whole community is collectively responsible, dealing with crime has become a private problem. Those with adequate resources have removed themselves from the violent confines of the inner city. The wealthier have moved to gated communities or guarded buildings or at least to houses with elaborate window guards, locks and alarms. Spending on private security measures has grown to several times the aggregate total of all public spending on criminal justice. There are twice as many private security personnel as public police officers.

So the burden of crime falls quite unequally on different sectors of the population. In a recent essay in *The Public Interest*, John DiIulio gathers a great deal of sobering evidence of this pattern. Black youngsters are now up to seven times more likely to be murdered than their white counterparts. In the late 1980s, a survey of seventy-five urban counties found that black citizens—only 20 percent of the population—accounted for more than half the murder victims. The disparities are every bit as dramatic when considered in geographic or class terms. The city of Philadelphia, for example, with only 14 percent of the population of Pennsylvania, accounts for 42 percent of violent crime in the state.

Far less striking disparities in the scale of school expenditures have provoked extensive litigation in many states. Far less striking disparities in employment patterns have provoked ambitious lawsuits, invoking statistics to "prove" unlawful discrimination, even where there is no evidence of deliberate malice. But disparities in susceptibility to violent crime have been shrugged off as a sad fact of life, for which public authorities bear no responsibility.

True, crime victims have not been entirely neglected. Some jurisdictions have experimented with "victim compensation programs," which try to extract compensation payments from the perpetrators. But there's rarely much to extract, and the programs hardly act as a strong deterrent to hardened criminals. Really bad riots, as in Los Angeles in 1992, may call forth federal disaster relief funds to soften the impact of the criminal devastation. But such payments, financed by federal taxpayers, have no direct connection to the responsibilities of local officials in the affected areas. None of these measures does anything to resist the trend by which affluent taxpayers wash their hands of the most crime-infested areas.

So federal pressure may be necessary to force states to provide more determined and equitable responses to crime. At this stage in our history, it can hardly be argued that the federal government lacks the constitutional authority to impose such pressures. As numerous Supreme Court rulings attest, Congress can make the states answerable to anything it chooses to call a "right" or to anything it judges appropriate for enforcing the Fourteenth Amendment guarantee of "equal protection of the laws." But to be effective, financial pressures must be properly calibrated. The model ought to be the state workmen's compensation systems, which are financed by employer payments and thus put continual pressure on employers to contain costs by improving safety. A program that simply requires states to offer token consolation payments to crime victims may be lost in the myriad of state welfare spending already in place. If, on the other hand, the program turns into a general social insurance scheme, there may be irresistible pressure to share the full cost among federal taxpayers at large—in which case it will cease to have any focused incentive effects on state crime-control measures.

Several forms of targeted liability are worth thinking about. First, the focus should be on crimes of violence rather than all crime; it's violent crime that drives middle-class people from cities. Second, there should be an effort to target gang violence (returning to the original Riot Act focus on violence committed by three or more people) and on offenses involving the use of guns. But, above all, there should be a focus on crimes committed by persons already convicted of violent offenses. States are under so much pressure to free up prison space that they commonly release dangerous offenders onto the streets. A recent survey by the Bureau of Justice Statistics found that almost one-quarter of murder arrestees were either on probation or parole; the figure for those arrested in connection with other violent offenses was even higher. Such reckless policies ought to have a cost—not merely to the victims.

Whatever the precise focus, there's an easy mechanism for enforcement: let state governments be liable for damages to the victims (or their families), just as damages are now awarded against private firms held responsible for injury, disablement or death. If someone is injured by violent crime, allow the victim (or his or her family) to pursue damage claims against the state for allowing this to happen.

The costs may quickly become rather substantial—more than enough to make politicians take notice. A recent survey of Wisconsin hospitals, for example, calculated that a shotgun assault victim may have to bear up to $5 million in lost income and medical expenses over a thirty-five-year working life in the aftermath of the crime. A 1993 study in *Health Affairs* calculated that in a three-year period at the end of the 1980s, violent crime imposed lifetime costs of $178 billion. Making states pay even a sizable fraction of such costs, in compensation payments to victims, will begin to bite rather quickly.

Would such costs make the whole undertaking prohibitively expensive? States are certainly in a better position to bear such costs than municipal governments. The feds might also share some of the costs to help states (even though the proposed new law against unfunded federal mandates does not apply to civil rights measures). And we may hope that, over time, better crime control will reduce the burden of compensation payments. But the key point is that victims are *already* bearing the costs of crime and the secondary effects of crime as it dampens investment, depresses real estate values and so on. The question is not whether we will "pay" for the costs of crime but whether we will try to spread the costs more equitably—and so focus taxpayer attention on the government's failure to do better in controlling it.

A system of state liability promises several striking advantages. First, it will not require any elaborate bureaucracy to administer, nor even require the contributions of the public interest bar or of special civil rights organizations. An army of tort lawyers can be readily enlisted to pursue the promise of damage awards. In the second place, this system can encourage greater participation in the criminal justice system by the victims of crime. Victims are often reluctant to come forward or cooperate with the police; it could lead to retaliation and involve unpleasantness and large amounts of time. Under the tort system, victims would have a direct financial incentive to get involved. Third, a system of this kind can leave wide discretion to the states (and their localities) to implement whatever crime-control measures they think best. It would open up competition for effective crime control tactics and provide a reliable gauge for how greatly any specific government is in default of its most basic obligation to citizens.

Congress decreed in the 1970s that states must secure certain standards of air and water quality. It decreed that cities must make buses, subways, sidewalks and public buildings accessible to wheelchairs. If it is proper to impose heavy financial burdens in the name of such modern amenities, it is surely reasonable to make the states accountable for their success in dealing with the first obligation of any and all governments—securing citizens from violence.

A CALL TO ARMS[6]

Yeah, I armed myself two years ago. Why? Because, like a lot of other Angelenos, I was scared. My 26-year-old son was shot in his car on Crescent Heights near Pico, taking the shortcut back from the airport. He got lucky. A Hollywood wound: just a crease in the arm—through his leather jacket and a slug lost in the dashboard. And my wife was having troubles, too. She works at a law firm in Santa Monica and was being stalked and badgered. Her fellow employees would herd together to go to the parking garage. Out there, they knew, were rapists, muggers, carjackers. I, too, was getting tired of looking over my shoulder for follow-home robbers every time I went to the market. One day, I almost ran over a man sprawled in my driveway, when I backed the car out. He was drunk or drugged, or maybe looking for an easy mark. Was my house a safe place? I felt uneasy even in Beverly Hills. Famous people were being held up at gunpoint outside of upscale restaurants. Let me tell you, I didn't want to be frightened. I wanted to be braver than that, to have some honor and dignity, even though I was still living in L.A. Then came the riots.

That's when Reginald Denny and I realized the police weren't going to be there for us.

Later, I learned how few police there are. It turns out there are only about 800 of them on the street at any one time. That's out of 8,000 or so. I found out they were overworked, underpaid and overwhelmed. That's 800 officers for some 10 million citizens. Not much chance they'd be on my doorstep when I needed them. So I decided to get trained in defensive firearms.

I had shot in the army, but that was 43 years back. I had even owned guns: a shotgun for bird shooting before I gave it up; a handgun stuck somewhere in the closet. Now, I felt an urgency.

I went to the American Pistol Institute in Arizona for a long, hard week. I worked out with California Pistolcraft Seminars in Los Angeles, starting at the beginning like the gray-haired lady next to me and continuing through intermediate and advanced courses. So, now I hold certificates, suitably engraved, that de-

[6]Article by Robert Dillon, screenwriter, from *Los Angeles* 39/4:53-55 Ap '94. Copyright © 1994 *Los Angeles*. Reprinted with permission.

clare my proficiency in defensive pistol, defensive shotgun and
police rifle. What this means is very real: I can draw from the hol-
ster, make two shots to center mass (read: chest) and one shot to
the central nervous system (read: head) in one and a half seconds.
I can hit a target at 50 yards with a government-issue .45 semiautomatic and sometimes make hits at the same target set at over
100 yards.

The important part is the one and a half seconds. That's the
same amount of time a bad guy with a knife needs to cover 19 feet
to stab you in the chest.

I also learned gun safety. I learned to treat every gun as if it
were loaded. I thought about the years before I was trained and
wondered how I survived them. I learned there's no such animal
as "accidental discharge." Guns don't go off by themselves, but
they can go off if mishandled. I worked especially hard on shoot/
no-shoot targets: Does he have a weapon? What's in his hand?
The one guy I don't want to be is the one who shoots a Japanese
exchange student waving his camera.

Once, I shot a target lurking behind a door. The target was
a mean, ugly blond guy sticking his gun in my face. Or so I
thought as I got off two hits, center mass. The instructor shook
his head. I looked again. The target was just pointing his thick,
ugly finger at me. I learned two lessons: Don't ever shoot unless
you're absolutely sure there's a weapon and a real threat, and
never point your finger at a man with a gun.

You should try to understand that I'm a registered Democrat.
I voted for Bill Clinton. I really consider myself a liberal. I believe
in social justice and most of the things in which liberals believe.
I'm not a member of the NRA, but I do believe that an honest,
well-trained, armed citizen isn't a bad thing to be.

Take the guns away from the criminals.

Sounds great, doesn't it? Maybe we could do it if we threw
away the Constitution. Maybe we could actually stop bad men
from stealing them or smuggling them or making them. Maybe
we could also take away their knives, lead pipes, sticks and rocks.
But maybe, even then, I wouldn't like to face down some Joe who
can bench-press 450 pounds, has a rap sheet six pages long and
has his hands on my wife's legs—not without an equalizer.

A citizen can carry a gun openly in Arizona. He can easily get
a permit to carry concealed in Florida. Except for the foreign visitor, whom bad guys know don't have a weapon, crime has gone

down in Florida. The message to criminals is: "Some people fight back."

Maybe if there had been a well-trained, armed civilian on the Long Island commuter train, he could have stopped Colin Ferguson from gunning down 6 people and wounding 17. Maybe someone could have stopped the massacre at McDonald's or shootings in post offices. There are numerous stories of civilians who have used their weapons against attackers and saved lives.

I look around. I think many honest citizens are already carrying guns. I suppose maybe some 50 percent of people in Los Angeles own guns. I guess maybe some 5 percent carry them. Well, that means there are 300,000 or 400,000 citizens, not crooks, out there carrying guns—and relatively responsibly. If they weren't, you'd have heard about it. All we get is the occasional actor caught with his 9-mm in his pants. The others go right on carrying. They'd rather face a weapons charge than be shot down on the street.

Sometimes, we get strange advice from our law enforcement. We're told to comply with a mugger's demands: Hand over your cash. But nowadays, they're shooting first and robbing second. What about the carjacker who says, "Get in the car"? Why is it we tell our children, if they're approached by a stranger, to thrash, kick, bite, scream, run away—do anything, but never, *never* get in that car? What's wrong with this picture? If kids are taught to fight back, why should any of us hand ourselves over to criminals?

I have a dear friend who hates the idea that I have a gun. My friend wants to ban all guns. So I asked my friend, "What if a bad guy gets into your house? Comes after your son? Comes after you?" My friend thinks about it and says, "If I had a gun, I wouldn't use it. I guess I'd just have to die." That just makes me feel sad. I want my friend to live. I want my friend to have the courage to fight.

Unlike the NRA, and closer to Bill Clinton's position, I believe that gun ownership should be licensed. I think owners must be trained in safety if they keep a gun in their home. But I also believe that a mentally competent, honest citizen, with training equal to or better than a sworn police officer's, should be allowed to carry a concealed defensive firearm. I think this kind of license should be renewed every couple of years. I think proficiency in safety and shooting should be demonstrated. And I think it would be a good thing for honest, law-abiding citizens to be so armed.

If the "militia" mentioned in the Second Amendment to the Constitution means anything, it means us.

It doesn't mean vigilantism. It sure doesn't mean seeking out criminals and shooting them down. It confers no police powers. Thank God we have the police to do it for us. What it does confer is the right to defend oneself, one's family, some innocent bystander, from a criminal in your home or an armed psycho on the street. Of course, a gun is not the only answer. It is not even the first line of self-defense—it should be the last resort, to be used only in the gravest extreme.

I wish someone would fix the crime problem. I wish it would go away. Sometimes, I think people in high places know how to fix it but don't have the will. It means giving up some long-held and cherished policies.

For me, the motor that's driving most of the street crime is our country's failed narcotics policy. I think it's time we took a second look. The amount of drug money leaving this country is some $40 billion a year. The amount spent on trying to control drugs is close to $150 billion. Wouldn't it be great to see that money spent on making jobs, improving education and medical treatment? For me, drugs are a social problem, not a criminal one. We could empty our crowded jails to make room for the violent criminal. We could make it a life sentence for those that sell drugs to kids.

America is an uncommon place, a place where freedoms still exist that other countries have given up. We hold a unique position in the world by virtue of our willingness to defend liberty. Take away personal liberty, and you take away that which makes us Americans: the ability to take responsibility for ourselves—including our own personal defense.

I sure don't want to see us get on the road to the overcontrol that's happened to other nations. I don't want us to end up like the English, French, Germans, or Japanese, where they put the safety of their skins before their liberty.

Many in this country would give up their own liberty for personal safety. It's not easy to live in freedom, because there's a price to pay, and that price is disorder. The only person ultimately responsible for you and your family's safety is yourself. That takes bravery—and maybe a gun.

In Los Angeles today, one should definitely be brave.

"DOES PRISON PAY?" REVISITED[7]

Returning to the Crime Scene

Several years ago, in these pages, we tried to referee an acrimonious debate between criminologists who insisted that prisons "cost too much" and those who responded that they "protect too little." Our contention was that both sides of the debate were stating their positions far too strongly given the lack of available empirical evidence. By presenting new survey data, we hoped to bring a little calm into the storm. But we succeeded only in changing the storm's direction—toward us. Shorn of most of our peacekeeping illusions, we are back to revisit the question, "Does prison pay?"—again by way of new survey data.

Our original offering was a cost-benefit analysis of imprisonment based on a 1990 prisoner self-report survey we conducted in Wisconsin. The survey, based on a sample of 6 percent of the state's prison population, found that in the year before their incarceration, half of the prisoners had committed 12 crimes or more, excluding drug crimes. Using the best available estimates of prison operating costs and the social costs of crime, we calculated that imprisoning 100 convicted felons who offended at the median rate cost $2.5 million, but that leaving them on the streets cost $4.6 million. We noted that for as much as a quarter of prisoners, other correctional options, such as probation, intensive drug treatment, or some other programs, might well be even more cost effective than imprisonment and we stressed the need for more research.

What we offer now is a new prisoner self-report survey, one that we conducted in New Jersey in 1993 of a random sample of 4 percent of recent male entrants to the state's prison population. Analysis of this survey reconfirms our earlier finding: prison pays for most state prisoners. Most state prisoners are either violent or repeat offenders who pose a real and present danger to the

[7]Article by Anne Morrison Piehl, assistant professor at the Kennedy School of Government, Harvard University and John J. DiIulio, Jr., professor at Princeton University, and director of the Brookings Center for Public Management, from *Brookings Review* 13/1:21-5 Ja '95. Copyright © 1995 by Brookings Institution Press. Reprinted with permission.

physical safety or property of any communities into which they might be released. For them, assuredly, prison pays. But prison does not pay for all prisoners. It does not pay for all convicted felons. Most emphatically, it does not pay for all convicted drug felons. The public and its purse could benefit if 10–25 percent of prisoners were under some other form of correctional supervision or released from custody altogether.

Most Prisoners Are Dangerous, Repeat Criminals

According to Lawrence A. Greenfeld of the U.S. Bureau of Justice Statistics, fully 94 percent of all state prisoners have either been convicted of a violent crime or been previously sentenced to probation or incarceration. Greenfeld's 94 percent statistic is unassailable. But even it understates the actual number and severity of crimes committed by state prisoners.

In the first place, adult prisoner profiles do not reflect the crimes committed by prisoners before they were of age to be legally tried, convicted, and sentenced as adults. Most state prisoners have long juvenile records, which are officially closed to adult authorities and are not considered by adult courts at sentencing time. According to our New Jersey survey, two out of three prisoners had served time in a juvenile institution. Other studies have shown that about 60 percent of youths aged 18 and under in long-term secure facilities have a history of violence. Many studies reveal that between a quarter and a third of juvenile criminals are high-rate offenders who commit a mix of violent and property crimes. Juveniles account for about a fifth of all weapons arrests and have set frightening new homicide records in the 1990s.

In a recent survey, 93 percent of judges in the juvenile system agreed that juvenile offenders should be fingerprinted, and 85 percent agreed that juvenile records should be open to adult authorities. As it now stands, however, juvenile crimes of assault, rape, robbery, burglary, and murder will mean nothing in adult courts and will not appear in statistical profiles of prisoners' criminality.

Second, more than 90 percent of all criminal cases do not go to trial because the offender pleads guilty to a lesser charge. Even violent crimes are routinely plea-bargained—an estimated 77 percent of rape cases, 85 percent of aggravated assault cases, and 87 percent of robbery cases. Unless one believes that all charges that are plea-bargained away are for crimes that the offender did not commit, then one must admit that actual crimes are swept under the criminal-records rug by plea bargaining. As yet no systematic empirical studies have estimated the deflationary effects of plea bargaining on the length and severity of prisoners' criminal records. But many prosecutors believe that the effects are large, and evidence is growing all around the country that they are right.

Third, as our two prisoner self-report surveys plainly reveal, most prisoners commit many times more nondrug felony crimes than they are ever arrested, convicted, and imprisoned for committing.

In the late 1970s the RAND Corporation conducted prisoner self-report surveys in Texas, Michigan, and California. Among other things, RAND's surveys showed that the median number of crimes, excluding all drug crimes, committed by prisoners the year before they were incarcerated was 15. In the late 1980s amidst the first round of controversies over benefit-cost analyses of imprisonment, some asserted that the RAND numbers could not even come close to being replicated in bigger-sample, more up-to-date surveys.

Both our prisoner self-report surveys were modeled on the RAND survey, though in both the sample was much larger. The 1993 New Jersey survey found that the median number of non-drug crimes committed by prisoners the year before their imprisonment was 12—exactly what it was for Wisconsin prisoners in 1990, and three lower than it was for prisoners in RAND surveys.

Although the exact replication is striking, future surveys will no doubt show that 12 is not a magic number. But serious analysts must now concede that there is less reason to be skeptical that the typical prisoner commits many undetected crimes, excluding drug crimes, the year before his incarceration.

In sum, the Greenfeld data alone are enough to rebut the notion that most state prisoners are petty, first-time, or mere drug offenders with few prior arrests, no previous convictions, no history of violence, and no potential for doing criminal harm if released tomorrow morning. And when we acknowledge that most prisoners commit crimes as juveniles, most prisoners plea bargain away crimes they have committed as adults, and most prisoners have committed a slew of undetected crimes the year before their incarceration, that notion is not only decidedly distorted but downright dangerous. It is a myth that anti-incarceration activists and their allies should be free to peddle, but that no responsible policymaker, prosecutor, judge, journalist, academic, or average citizen can afford to buy.

Calculating Social Costs

Estimating the social costs and benefits of competing transportation or environmental policies is no analytical picnic. But estimating them for imprisonment and other sentencing options is a certain analytical migraine.

For starters, it is widely asserted that it costs $25,000 to keep a prisoner behind bars for a year. But the latest Bureau of Justice Statistics figures for average annual spending per prisoner are $15,586 for the states and $14,456 for the federal Bureau of Prisons (which holds about 10 percent of all prisoners). These figures are calculated by dividing the total spent on salaries, wages, supplies, utilities, transportation, contractual services, and other current operating expenses by the average daily inmate population.

But hidden and indirect costs of running prisons might bring the $25,000 figure closer to reality than the official spending averages would allow. For example, some tiny but nontrivial fraction of government workers outside of corrections (human services, central budgeting offices) spend time on matters pertaining to prisoners. And Harvard economist Richard Freeman and others suggest that incarceration decreases post-release employability and lifetime earnings potential. Thus an ideal estimate of the social costs of imprisonment would include any relevant spending by other government agencies, plus whatever public unemployment compensation, welfare, and health expenditures result from the negative short- and long-term labor market effects of imprisonment on ex-prisoners.

Also, there is wide inter- and intra-system variation not only in what it costs to operate prisons, but in how prison dollars are allocated as between security functions (uniformed custodial staff), basic services (food, heat, medical supplies), treatment programs, recreational facilities, plant maintenance, and other expenditures. Whatever the best estimate of prison operating costs, such cost differences suggest that efficiency losses are occurring in some places and that efficiency gains are possible in others.

The cost-effectiveness of prisons, however, is by no means strictly determined by correctional administrators. Over the past 25 years the courts have had a major impact on both the total costs of operating prisons and the distribution of prison dollars between security and other needs. For example, in the wake of a sweeping court order, prison operating costs in Texas grew from $91 million in 1980 to $1.84 billion in 1994, a tenfold increase in real terms, while the state's prison population barely doubled. Texas is now one of at least 20 states that spends less than half of every prison dollar on security.

Finally, it is worth remembering that barely a penny of every federal, state, and local tax dollar goes to support state prisons and local jails. State and local governments spend 15 times what the federal government spends on corrections. But state and local spending on prisons and jails amounts to only $80.20 per capita a year, or $1.54 per capita a week.

Estimating Social Benefits

Whatever the best estimate of how much it costs society to keep a convicted criminal behind bars for a year, how do we decide whether it's worth the money? Imprisonment offers at least four types of social benefits. The first is retribution: imprisoning Peter punishes him and expresses society's desire to do justice. Second is deterrence: imprisoning Peter may deter either him or Paul or both from committing crimes in the future. Third is rehabilitation: while behind bars, Peter may participate in drug treatment or other programs that reduce the chances that he will return to crime when free. Fourth is incapacitation: from his cell, Peter can't commit crimes against anyone save other prisoners, staff, or visitors.

At present, it is harder to measure the retribution, deterrence, or rehabilitation value of imprisonment to society than it is to measure its incapacitation value. The types of opinion surveys and data sets that would enable one to arrive at meaningful estimates of the first three social benefits of imprisonment simply do not yet exist.

Thus, we focus exclusively on the social benefits of imprisonment measured in terms of its incapacitation value. As columnist Ben Wattenberg so vividly put it, everyone grasps that "A thug in prison can't shoot your sister." Thus, if a given crime costs its victims and society X dollars in economic and other losses (hospital bills, days out of work, physical pain, and emotional anguish), and if we know that, when free, a convicted criminal commits Y such crimes per year, then the yearly social benefits of imprisoning him are equal to X times Y. If we accept that it costs $25,000 to imprison this convicted criminal for a year, then the benefit-cost ratio of imprisoning him is equal to the product of X times Y divided by $25,000. If the ratio is greater than 1, then the social benefits exceed the costs and "prison pays" for this offender; but if the ratio is lower than 1, then the social costs exceed the benefits and it does not pay to keep him locked up.

But remember: we are monetizing the social benefits solely in terms of imprisonment's incapacitation value. Because there is every reason to suppose that the retribution, deterrence, and rehabilitation values of imprisonment are each greater than zero— that is, because it is virtually certain that in addition to incapacitating criminals who would commit crimes when free, prison also succeeds in punishing, deterring, and rehabilitating at least some prisoners under some conditions—our estimate of the net social benefits of imprisonment is bound to be an *under*estimate. And if, therefore, our estimate measured only in terms of prison's incapacitation value is positive, it means that the actual social benefits of imprisonment are even higher and that prison most definitely pays.

Several recent advances have been made in measuring the costs of crime to victims and society. For example, a recent Bureau of Justice Statistics study reports a total of 33.6 million criminal victimizations in 1992. The study estimated that in 1992 crime victims lost $17.2 billion in direct costs—losses from theft or property damage, cash losses, medical expenses, and lost pay from work.

But the BJS estimate did not include direct costs (for example, medical costs) to victims incurred six months or more after the crime. Nor did it include decreased work productivity, the less tangible costs of pain and suffering, increased insurance premiums and moving costs due to victimization, and other indirect costs.

A 1993 study by Ted R. Miller and others in *Health Affairs* took a more comprehensive view of the direct costs of crime and included some indirect costs as well. The study estimated the costs and monetary value of lost quality of life in 1987 due to death and injuries, both physical and psychological, resulting from violent crime. Using various measures, the study estimated that each murder costs $2.4 million, each rape $60,000, each arson $50,000, each assault $25,000, and each robbery $19,000. The estimated total cost over the lifetime of the victims of all violent crimes committed during 1987–90 was $178 billion per year, or many times the BJS estimate of direct economic costs.

Even these estimates, however, omit the detailed cost accounting of site-specific, crime-specific studies. For example, a recent survey of admissions to Wisconsin hospitals over a 41-month period found that 1,035 patients were admitted for gunshot wounds caused by assaults. These patients accumulated more than $16 million in hospital bills, about $6.8 million of it paid by taxes. Long-term costs rise far higher. For example, just one shotgun assault victim in the survey was likely to incur costs of more than $5 million in lost income and medical expenses over the next 35 years.

Likewise, several studies have estimated the number of crimes averted by incapacitating criminals. For example, BJS statistician Patrick J. Langan has shown that in 1989 an estimated 66,000 fewer rapes, 323,000 fewer robberies, 380,000 fewer assaults, and 3.3 million fewer burglaries were attributable to the difference between the crime rates of 1973 and those of 1989. As Langan has observed, if only one-half or one-quarter of the reductions were due to rising incarceration rates, that would still leave prisons responsible for sizable reductions in crime. Also he has estimated that tripling the prison population from 1975 to 1989 reduced reported and unreported violent crime by 10–15 percent below what it would otherwise have been, thereby preventing a conservatively estimated 390,000 murders, rapes, robberies, and aggravated assaults in 1989 alone.

Results of the New Jersey Study

What can the New Jersey prisoner self-report survey contribute to a cost-benefit analysis of imprisonment? . . . For each offender in the New Jersey sample we multiplied these amounts by the annualized number of offenses reported of each type. . . . The median social cost of crime was about $70,098. In other words, half of the prisoners in the sample inflicted more costs on society and half less than $70,098. The social cost associated with the prisoner in the 25th percentile (that is, 75 percent of the sample inflicted higher social costs than he did) was about $19,509, and at the 10th percentile it was $1,650.

. . . Dividing the median social cost per crime of $70,098 by $25,000 yields a benefit-cost ratio of 2.80: for every dollar it costs to keep a median-offending prisoner behind bars society saves at least $2.80 in the social costs of crimes averted.

The prisoner at the 25th percentile was essentially a high-rate property offender, reporting that he committed auto thefts at a rate of three a year, burglaries at a rate of six a year, and petty thefts at a rate of 24 a year. Dividing the total social cost of these crimes by the cost of incarceration yields a benefit-cost ratio of 0.78. And at the 10th percentile, the ratio is a clearly cost-ineffective zero.

Just Say No to No Parole

Clearly, the social benefits of incapacitating criminals, however great they may be, are nonetheless subject to the law of diminishing returns.

Make no mistake: within three years of their community-based sentences about half of all probationers either abscond or are returned to prison for a new crime, while roughly half of all parolees are convicted of a new crime. Of the 5 million people under correctional supervision in this country at any given time, 72 percent are not incarcerated. Even violent offenders serve barely 40 percent of their sentences in confinement. Each year community-based felons commit millions of crimes, many violent, that could have been prevented if they had been imprisoned for all or most of their terms.

But efforts, in Virginia and elsewhere, to abolish parole are too tough by half. For while about half of all parolees recidivate, the other half do not. Nationally, each year we spend more than 7.5 times more on prisons and jails (which house 28 percent of offenders) than we do on probation and parole (which account for the remaining 72 percent) combined. Thus we spend more than 20 times as much to hold each prisoner as we do to supervise each community-based offender. No doubt a large fraction of the parole population should be imprisoned. But a no-parole policy lowers rather than increases the chances that the system will sort offenders cost-effectively.

This is especially true where drug offenders are concerned. Between 1980 and 1992 the fraction of new state prisoners whose most serious conviction offense was a drug offense rose from 6.8 percent to 30.5 percent. Does that mean that one-third of the prison population consists of "mere drug offenders"? By no means. The vast majority of this group are recidivists with many a nondrug felony on their rap sheets, to say nothing of juvenile crimes, crimes they plea-bargained away, and crimes they got away with completely.

Then what fraction of prisoners might be accurately characterized as "drug-only offenders," meaning offenders whose only adult crimes have been drug crimes? At this point we have no way of knowing. But about 27 percent of the New Jersey sample reported that in the four months before incarceration their *only* offenses were drug sales. Nearly a quarter said they first got involved in crime to get money for drugs. And 3 percent were convicted of drug possession and reported no other crimes.

To be consistent methodologically, we must consider the incapacitation benefits of incarcerating such a substantial population. Doing so dramatically changes the results and the implications of our analysis. We believe that the best estimate of the incapacitation effect (number of drug sales prevented by incarcerating a drug dealer) is zero, and therefore value drug crimes (sales and possession) at zero social cost. Other analysts, including many whom no one can accuse of being soft on drug crime or in favor of drug legalization, have reached similar conclusions. For example, in a recent issue of *Commentary*, James Q. Wilson observed that prison terms for crack dealers "do not have the same incapacitative effect as sentences for robbery . . . [A] drug dealer sent away is replaced by a new one because an opportunity has opened up." Many law enforcement and corrections officials have reached the same conclusion.

. . . Including drug offenders in our analysis lowers the cost-effectiveness of incarceration across the board: even at the median, imprisonment appears to be very expensive. If even half of the inmates who report that their only crime was selling drugs are telling the truth, then 15 percent of New Jersey's spending on prisons is being devoted to "sending a message" about drug dealing. We are open to convincing evidence that the public is willing to pay substantial sums for retribution against drug dealers. And we are aware that certain types of prison-based drug treatment programs can work to reduce the chances that an offender will return to drugs or crime upon release. But let no one suppose that by incarcerating most drug offenders we succeed in averting lots of drug crimes. If there is an empirically sound argument for a no-parole policy that makes no distinctions between drug-only offenders and other prisoners, we have yet to hear it.

Forging a New Consensus?

When we first ventured into the "Does prison pay?" debate, we were struck by the absence of empirical data to buttress the large claims being made on both sides. Now more than ever we are convinced that the path to a new intellectual consensus in this area, as in crime policy generally, can be paved not by disagreeing more amicably about the implications of what is already known (though that could be a pleasant change), but by agreeing more fully about the gaps in our knowledge and how best to fill them.

For example, many want drug-only offenders locked up regardless of the questionable incapacitation or general deterrence benefits of doing so. Likewise, others want to legalize drugs outright. But honest minds on both sides must admit that we do not yet have a definitive estimate of the fraction of the prison population that consists of drug-only offenders.

Little by little analysts are beginning to sketch a picture of the amount and severity of crimes committed by prisoners when free and to explain the conditions under which some community-based felons succeed in staying drug- and crime-free. But we need a much fuller picture, a much clearer explanation.

In short, a new intellectual consensus on crime policy can be built not by avoiding the hardest policy-relevant empirical questions, but by attempting to identify and answer them, preferably in common with those with whom we are now most inclined to disagree strongly. Through a new Brookings research project, we hope to help foster just such a consensus.

WHY YOU CAN HATE DRUGS AND
STILL WANT TO LEGALIZE THEM[8]

There's no breeze, only bare, stifling heat, but Kevin can scarcely support his wispy frame. He bobs forward, his eyes slowly closing until he drifts asleep, in a 45-degree hunch. "Kevin?" I say softly. He jerks awake and slowly rubs a hand over his spindly chest. "It's so hot in here I can hardly think," he says.

Kevin is wearing an "Americorps" baseball cap, and I ask him where he got it. The lids close over his glassy eyes and then open again, showing a look of gentle, but deep confusion. He removes the hat, revealing hair the tone of a red shirt that's been through the washer a thousand times. He blinks again and glances at the cap. He has no idea.

This July I spent a long, hot day talking to junkies in New York City, in a run-down hotel near Columbia University. Some, like Kevin, were reticent. Others spoke freely about their lives and addictions. I sat with Melissa for 20 minutes as she patiently hunted her needle-scarred legs for a vein to take a spike. She had just fixed after a long dry spell. "I was sick," she told me. "I could hardly move. And Papo"—she gestures toward a friend sitting across from her—"he helped me out. He gave me something to make me better."

To most Americans, addicts like Kevin and Melissa and Papo are not people, but arguments. Some victims of drug use inspire sympathy, or irritation, or just plain worry. But it is the junkies—seemingly bereft of humanity, subsisting in what one former addict calls "soul-death"—who justify our national attitude toward certain drugs: that they should be illegal, unavailable, and totally suppressed.

But this country has another drug problem, one with its own tragic stories. In 1993, Launice Smith was killed in a shoot-out between rival drug dealers at a football game at an elementary school in Washington, D.C. There were four other murder victims in the same neighborhood that day. Launice stood out, though, because she was only four years old.

[8]Article by Joshua Wolf Shenk from *The Washington Monthly* 27/10:32-7 O '95. Copyright © by The Washington Monthly Company, Washington D.C. Reprinted with permission.

Addicts suffer from illegal drugs. But each year hundreds of children like Launice are killed *because* drugs are illegal. It's difficult, but crucial, to understand this distinction. By turning popular drugs into illegal contraband, prohibition sparks tremendous inflation. Small amounts of plant leaves and powder that cost only pennies to grow and process sell for hundreds of dollars on the street. All told, the black market in this country takes in $50 to $60 billion in income each year. In lawful society, such a large industry would be regulated by rules and enforcement mechanisms. But the intense competition of the black market is regulated only by violence. Rival entrepreneurs don't go to the courts with a dispute. They shoot it out in the street.

The black market now holds entire communities in its grip. In addition to the violence—and crime driven by addicts supporting expensive habits—the fast cash of dealing lures many young people away from school, into the drug trade, and often onto a track toward jail or death.

We are caught, then, between the Kevins and the Launices, between the horror of drug abuse and the horror of the illegal drug trade. Making drugs legally available, with tight regulatory controls, would end the black market, and with it much of the violence, crime, and social pathology we have come to understand as "drug-related." And yet, history shows clearly that lifting prohibition would allow for more drug use, and more abuse and addiction.

I spent that day in New York to face this excruciating dilemma. It's easy to call for an end to prohibition from an office in Washington, D.C. What about when looking into Kevin's dim eyes, or confronting the images of crack babies, shriveled and wincing?

The choice between two intensely unpleasant options is never easy. But, considering this problem in all its depth and complexity, it becomes clear that drug prohibition does more harm than good. We can't discount the problem of drug abuse (and that includes the abuse of legal drugs). But prohibition didn't keep Kevin from becoming an addict in the first place, and it certainly isn't helping him stop. High prices for drugs do discourage some would-be users, though far fewer than the government would like. The fact is we have done a very poor job discouraging drug use with the blunt force of law. The hundreds of billions of dollars spent on drug control in the last several decades have yielded

only a moderate decline in the casual use of marijuana and cocaine. But there has been no decrease in hard-core addiction.
The total amount of cocaine consumed per capita has actually ris-
en. And even casual use is now creeping up.

Government does have a responsibility to limit the individual
and social costs of drug use, but such efforts must be balanced
against the harm they cause. And ending the drug war needn't
mean a surrender to addiction, or an affirmation of reckless drug
use. President Clinton's stance on cigarette addiction—that cigarettes can be both legal and tightly regulated, particularly with
respect to advertising aimed at children—points to a middle
ground. Potentially, we could do a *better* job of fighting drug
abuse, while avoiding the vicious side-effects of an outright ban.

Comparing the Costs

Unfortunately, this country's discussion of "the drug
problem" is marked by little clear analysis and much misinforma-
tion. Politicians and bureaucrats minimize or entirely ignore the
consequences of prohibition. At the other extreme, libertarians
call for government to withdraw from regulating intoxicants entirely. The press, meanwhile, does little to illuminate the costs
and benefits of the current prohibition or our many other policy
options. "We don't cover drug policy, except episodically as a
cops and robbers story," says Max Frankel, the recently retired
executive editor of *The New York Times*. He calls his paper's coverage of the subject "one of my failures there as an editor, and a failure of newspapers generally."

It's not that the consequences of prohibition can't be seen in
the newspapers. In the *Times*, for example, Isabel Wilkerson
wrote a stirring profile of Jovan Rogers, a Chicago crack dealer
who entered the trade when he was 14 and ended up crippled by
gunshot wounds. But Wilkerson, as reporters usually do, con-
veyed the impression that the pathology of the black market is unfortunate, but inevitable—not the result of policies that we can
change.

In fact, Rogers' story is a vivid display of the lethal drug trade
that prohibition creates, the temptation of bright young men,
and the cycle of destruction that soon follows.

For his first job, Rogers got $75 a day to watch out for the
police. Soon, he was earning thousands a day. And though Rogers

said he began dealing to support his family—"If there's nothing to eat at night," he asked, "who's going to go buy something to make sure something is there? I was the only man in the house"—the big bucks also seized him where, like most teenagers, he was most vulnerable. "If you sell drugs, you had anything you wanted," he said. "Any girl, any friend, money, status. If you didn't, you got no girlfriend, no friends, no money. You're a nothing."

This story is all too common. In communities where two-thirds of the youth lack the schooling or skills to get a decent job, drug dealing is both lucrative and glamorous. Rich dealers are role models and images of entrepreneurial success—the Bill Gateses of the inner city. Unlike straight jobs, though, dealing drugs means entering a world of gruesome violence. Like all initiates, Rogers was issued a gun, and learned quickly to shoot—to discipline other dealers in the gang or to battle rival gangs for control over a corner or neighborhood. Sometimes he would shoot blindly, out of raw fear. Newspapers report stories of "drug-related" murder. But drug *war* murder is more like it. The illegal drug trade is the country's leading cause of death by homicide—and the illegal drug trade wouldn't exist without prohibition.

Although it is popular these days to blame welfare for undermining the work ethic, often overlooked is the role played by the black market's twisted incentives, which lure men away from school and legitimate work—and, often, away from their families. In a recent two-page spread, *The Washington Post* celebrated successful students at the city's Eastern High School. Of the 76 students pictured, 64 were women—only 12 were men. The school's principal, Ralph Neal, acknowledges the role of the drug trade with a sigh, calling it a "tremendous temptation."

Writ large, the black market eventually consumes entire neighborhoods. At one time, the area of Philadelphia now referred to as "Badlands" was peppered with factories, mom-and-pop grocery stores, taverns, and theaters. Now drug dealers are positioned on street corners and in flashy cars, poised to fire their guns at the slightest provocation. Crack vials and dirty needles line the streets. Often, customers drive through in BMWs with New Jersey plates, making their buys and then scurrying back to the suburbs.

Of course, impoverished communities like this one have more troubles than just drug prohibition. But it is the black market, residents will tell you, that is a noose around their neck. Drive-by shootings and deadly stray bullets are bad enough, but some of the most devastating casualties are indirect ones. This summer two children suffocated while playing in an abandoned car in Southeast Washington. The kids avoided local playgrounds, one child said, because they feared "bullies and drug dealers."

"Kids in the inner city are scared to go to school," says Philippe Bourgois, a scholar who recently spent three and a half years with drug dealers in East Harlem writing *In Search of Respect: Selling Crack in El Barrio.* "You're going to pass five or six dealers hawking vials of crack on your way there. You face getting mugged in the hallway. The dealers . . . they drop out, but they don't stop going to school—that's where the action is."

A D.C. public school teacher told me that 13-year-old dealers, already fully initiated into the drug culture, crawl through a hole in the fence around her school's playground to talk to fifth and sixth graders. Once, after she and a security guard chased them off, a group of young dealers found her in the school's parking lot. "There's that snitching bitch," one kid said. "That's the bitch that snitched. I'm going to kill you, you snitching bitch." The drug war's Dr. Seuss.

A Nation Behind Bars

The high prices caused by prohibition drive crime in another way: Addicts need cash to feed their habits. The junkies I met in New York told me they would spend between $200 and $600 a week for drugs. Melissa, for example, once had a good job and made enough to pay her bills and to buy dope. Then she got laid off and turned to prostitution to support her habit. Others steal to pay for their drugs—from liquor stores, from their families, from dealers, or from other addicts. According to a study by the Bureau of Justice Statistics, one out of every three thefts are committed by people seeking drug money.

This crime wave does not restrict itself to the inner cities. Addicts seeking money to get a fix are very fond of the fine appliances and cash-filled wallets found in wealthier neighborhoods. Suburban high schools may not have swarms of dealers crawling through the fences, but dealers are there too. In fact, the suburbs are increasingly popular for dealers looking to take up residence.

Quite apart from the costs of the black market—the crime, the neighborhoods and lives ruined—Americans also pay a heavy price for the drug war itself. For fiscal 1996, Clinton has requested $14.6 billion for drug control (up from only $1.3 billion in 1983). State and local governments spend about twice that each year.

But these budgets reflect only a small portion of the costs. In 1980, the United States had 330,000 people in jail; today, it's well over a million, and drug offenders account for 46 percent of that increase. On top of the cost of building prisons, it takes more than $30,000 per year to keep someone in jail. Naturally, prison spending has exploded. The country now spends nearly $30 billion annually on corrections. Between 1970 and 1990, state and local governments hiked prison spending by 232 percent.

Even worse, thanks to mandatory minimum sentences, the system is overloaded with non-violent drug users and dealers, who now often receive harsher penalties than murderers, rapists, and serious white collar criminals. Solicited by an undercover DEA agent to find a cocaine supplier, Gary Fannon facilitated the deal and received a sentence of life without parole. Larry Singleton raped a teenager, hacked off her arms between the wrist and elbow, and left her for dead in the desert. He received the 14-year maximum sentence and served only eight years. This disparity is not the exception in modern law enforcement. It is the rule. Non-violent drug offenders receive an average 60 months in jail time, *five times* the average 12-month-sentence for manslaughter convicts.

Some people may say: Build more jails. In an era of tax cuts and fiscal freezes, though, every dollar spent on corrections comes from roads, or health care, or education. Even with the huge growth in prison spending, three-fourths of all state prisons were operating over their maximum capacity in 1992. Even conservatives like Michael Quinlan, director of the federal Bureau of Prisons under Reagan and Bush, have had enough of this insanity. "They're locking up a lot of people who are not serious or violent offenders," he says. "That . . . brings serious consequences in terms of our ability to incarcerate truly violent criminals."

If sticking a drug dealer in jail meant fewer dealers on the street, perhaps this wave of incarceration would eventually do some good. But it doesn't work like that: Lock up a murderer, and you have one less murderer on the street. Lock up a dealer, and you create a job opening. It's like jailing an IBM executive; the pay is good, the job is appealing, so someone will move into the office before long. Clearing dealers from one neighborhood only means they'll move to another. Busting a drug ring only makes room for a competitor. "We put millions of drug offenders through the courts—and we have more people in jail per capita than any country except Russia—but we're not affecting the drug trade, let alone drug use," says Robert Sweet, U.S. district judge in the Southern district of New York.

"It's perfectly obvious," Sweet says, "that if you took the money spent housing drug offenders and enforcing the drug laws, and apply it to straight law enforcement, the results would be very impressive." Indeed, what politicians ignore is all too clear to judges, prosecutors, and cops. "The drug war can't be won," says Joseph McNamara, the former chief of police in Kansas City and San Jose, who also spent 10 years on the New York City force. "Any cop will tell you that."

What makes it even tougher for law enforcement is the pervasiveness of corruption spawned by the black market in drugs. In May 1992, New York City police uncovered the largest corruption scandal in the department's 146-year history, most of it, according to the commission that investigated it, involving "groups of officers . . . identifying drug sites; planning raids; forcibly entering and looting drug trafficking locations, and sharing proceeds." There have been similar stories recently in Philadelphia, Washington, D.C., New Orleans, and Atlanta. Sadly, in movies like *The Bad Lieutenant*, art is imitating life. Cops shake down dealers, steal their cash, and sometimes deal the drugs themselves. Or they take bribes to protect dealers from arrest.

Despite these drug war casualties—and the dismal progress in stemming drug use—each year the war intensifies. Politicians from Newt Gingrich to Bill Bradley now push for expanding the death penalty for dealers. But experience shows that the deterrent effect will be negligible. "There is no evidence that increasing penalties for drug dealing deters people from doing it," says Quinlan. "It just doesn't work like that—not when your chances of getting caught are so low, and the profits are so high." As Quinlan points out, the D.E.A. and White House count it as a success if drug prices are driven up, but that only makes the problem worse. On the streets, meanwhile, we have the worst of both worlds: Drugs are expensive enough to fuel a deadly black market, but people still buy them.

Illegal drugs, left unregulated, are also much more dangerous than they need to be. Imagine drinking whisky with no idea of its potency. It could be 30 proof or 190 proof—or diluted with a dangerous chemical. One addict I met, Mary, had blood-red sores running up her arms—from cocaine cut with meat tenderizer. Virtually all "overdose" deaths from the use of illegal drugs are due to contaminants or the user's ignorance of the drug's potency. "Just deserts," one might say. But isn't the basis of our drug policy supposed to be concern for people's health and well-being?

Unfortunately, this country's leaders have lost sight of that principle. "Policies," Thomas Sowell has written, "are judged by their consequences, but crusades are judged by how good they make the crusaders feel." Drug prohibition is very much of a crusade, discussed in moral terms, supported on faith, not evidence. The DEA stages high-profile drug raids—covered dutifully in newspapers and magazines—but is never able to limit supply. The government sends troops to burn poppy in South America and stubbornly insists, despite overwhelming evidence to the contrary, that interdiction can make a real difference in keeping drugs out of the country.

Meanwhile, drug treatment—no panacea, but certainly more effective in limiting drug use than law enforcement or interdiction—is continually underfunded. Candidate Clinton promised "treatment on demand" in 1992, but President Clinton has not delivered. Like Reagan and Bush, he has spent about two-thirds of the anti-drug budget on law enforcement and interdiction.

For a real blood boiler, consider the case of pregnant women addicted to drugs. Lee Brown, White House director of drug policy control, often talks of visiting crack babies in the hospital to shame those who would liberalize drug laws. But, like many addicts, pregnant women often avoid treatment or health care because they fear arrest.

Although it's hard to believe, those who do seek help—for themselves and their unborn children—are often turned away. David Condliffe, who was the director of drug policy for New York City in the late eighties, conducted a survey that found that 85 percent of poor, pregnant crack addicts looking for treatment were refused everywhere they tried. Nationwide, treatment is available for only 10 percent of the 300,000 pregnant women who abuse illegal drugs. This is perhaps the greatest moral horror of our current policy—and it should shame everyone from President Clinton on down.

Beyond the Crusade

Regardless of your stance on drug policy, there can be no disagreement that we must demand honesty from public officials on this subject. Forget for a moment reporters' nonfeasance in covering the nuances of drug policy. When it comes to the drug war, they're also failing to expose coverups and outright lies.

As just one example, consider the case of needle exchange. Forty percent of new AIDS cases reported in 1992 (24,000 in total) came from infection through use of dirty needles. But the federal government continues to ban the use of AIDS-prevention funds for programs that replace dirty needles with clean ones.

This despite the fact that in 1994 the Centers for Disease Control issued a report concluding that needle exchange *does not* encourage heroin use, but *does* dramatically reduce HIV transmission. The report explicitly recommends that the federal ban be lifted. The Clinton Administration suppressed the report, but a copy finally leaked. Now, officials deny its basic finding. "[The CDC] pointed out that the jury is still out on needle exchange," Lee Brown told me. Either he hasn't read the report, or he is lying.

Even more infuriating, supporters of the drug war insist on confusing the harms of drug use with the harms of prohibition. William Bennett, for example, cites "murder and mayhem being committed on our cities' streets" as justification to intensify the drug war, when, as Milton Friedman wrote in an open letter to Bennett, "the very measures you favor are a major source of the evils you deplore." Meanwhile, in the current political climate, the likes of Joycelyn Elders—who merely suggested we *study* the link between prohibition and violence—are shouted down.

Facing Drug Abuse

Cocaine can cause heart attacks in people prone to irregular heartbeats, such as basketball star Len Bias, and seizures in people with mild epilepsy; it's even more dangerous mixed with alcohol and other drugs. Heroin can lead to intense physical dependence—withdrawal symptoms include nausea, convulsions, and loss of bowel control. Even marijuana can be psychologically addictive; smoking too much dope can lead to respiratory problems or even cancer.

Illegal drugs have social costs as well. Consistent intoxication—whether it's a gram-a-day coke fiend, or a regular pot smoker with a miserable memory—can mean lost productivity, increased accidents, and fractured relationships.

And addiction . . . well, it's not pretty. Coke addicts often suffer acute depression without a fix. Heroin is even worse. David Morrison, recalling his furious struggle with heroin addiction in *Washington City Paper*, describes the misery of waiting for his dealer: "If sweet oblivion is the initial carrot, savage withdrawal is the enduring stick. In time, the dope fiend is not so much chasing a high as fleeing a debacle."

Given the terrible consequences of drug abuse, any reasonable person is bound to object: How could we even consider making drugs generally available? But have you asked why alcohol and tobacco are kept generally available?

Tobacco products—linked to cancer of the lungs, throat, larynx, and ovaries—cause 30 percent of all cancer deaths. Even more tobacco-related deaths come from heart attacks and strokes. Every year 435,000 Americans die premature deaths because of cigarettes. And, of course, nicotine is extremely addictive: The Surgeon General has found that the "capture" rate— the percentage of people who become addicted after trying it—is higher with cigarettes than any other drug, legal or illegal. Most nicotine addicts are hooked before age 18.

Alcohol is even more destructive. Extensive drinking often results in bleeding ulcers, cirrhosis of the liver, stomach and intestinal inflammation, and muscle damage as well as severe damage to the brain and nervous system, manifested by blackouts and psychotic episodes.

As for social costs, alcohol is the most likely of all mind-altering substances to induce criminal behavior, according to the National Institute of Justice. Close to 11 million Americans are alcoholics, and another 7 million are alcohol abusers—meaning they've screwed up at work, been in an accident, or been arrested because of drinking. Drunk driving is the cause of a third of all traffic fatalities. Alcohol-related problems affect one out of every four American homes, and alcoholism is involved in 60 percent of all murders and 38 percent of child abuse cases. These statistics only confirm our everyday experience. Who doesn't know of a family shattered by an alcoholic, or someone who has suffered with an alcoholic boss?

The reason that alcohol and tobacco are legal, despite the damage they do, is that prohibition would be even worse. In the case of alcohol, we know from experience. The prohibition from 1919 to 1933 is now synonymous with violence, organized crime, and corruption. Financed by huge profits from bootlegging, gangsters like Al Capone terrorized cities and eluded the best efforts of law enforcement. It soon became too much.

After prohibition's repeal, consumption rates for alcohol did in fact rise. But as anyone who was alive in 1933 could tell you, the increase was hardly an explosion. And it seems likely that the rise was fueled by advertising and the movies. Drunks were likeable (bit-player Jack Norton played the amiable falling-down drunk in scores of movies of that era) or even glamorous (like William Powell in *The Thin Man* films). It took years for government, the media, and entertainers to realize their responsibility to push temperance—and even now they're not doing all they can.

BIBLIOGRAPHY

An asterisk (*) preceding a reference indicates that the article or part of it has been reprinted in this book.

BOOKS AND PAMPHLETS

Albanese, Jay S. White collar crime in America. Prentice Hall. '95.

⸺. & Pursley, Robert D. Crime in America: some existing and emerging issues. Regents/Prentice Hall. '93.

Bachman, Roney. Death and violence on the reservation: homicide, family violence, and suicide in American Indian populations. Suburn House. '92.

Bennett, Georgette. Crimewarps: the future of crime in America. Anchor Books. '87.

Bright, Jon. Crime prevention in America: a British perspective. University of Illinois at Chicago. Office of International Criminal Justice. '92.

Chin, Ko-lin. Chinese subculture and criminality: non-traditional crime groups in America. Greenwood. '90.

Doyle, Roger. The atlas of contemporary America: portrait of a nation—politics, economy, environment, ethnic and religious diversity, health issues, demographic patterns, quality of life, crime, personal freedoms. Facts on File. '94.

Flowers, Ronald B. Demographics and criminality: the characteristics of crime in America. Greenwood. '89.

Fox, Stephen R. Blood and power: organized crime in twentieth-century America. Penguin. '90.

Goldfarb, Ronald L. Perfect villains, imperfect heroes: Robert F. Kennedy's war against organized crime. Random House. '95.

Gurr, Ted Robert, ed. Violence in America. Sage. '89.

Kenney, Dennis Jay & Finckenauer, James O. Organized crime in America. Wadsworth. '95.

Keve, Paul W. Crime control and justice in America: searching for facts and answers. American Library Association. '95.

LeMay, Craig L. & Dennis, Everette E., eds. The culture of crime. Transaction. '95.

Meltzer, Milton. Crime in America. Morrow. '90.

Mizell, Louis R., Jr. Street sense for parents: keeping your child safe in a dangerous world. Berkley. '95.

Morgan, Kathleen O'Leary & Morgan, Scott, eds. City crime rankings. Morgan Quinto Corp. '95.

Olamigoke, Olumide K. How to reduce crime rates in America. American Literary. '94.

Parker, Steve. The drug war. Gloucester. '90.

Rohr, Janelle, ed. Violence in America: opposing viewpoints. Greenhaven. '90.

Rosenberg, Mark L. & Fenley, Mary Ann, eds. Violence in America a public health approach. Oxford University Press:UK. '91.

Schaum, Melita & Parrish, Karen. Stalked: breaking the silence on the crime of stalking in America. Pocket. '95.

Sheley, Joseph F. & Wright, James D. In the line of fire: youth, guns, and violence in urban America. Aldine de Gruyter. '95.

Tanner, Mack. The armed-citizen solution to crime in the streets: so many criminals, so few bullets. Paladin. '95.

Territo, Leonard, James Halsted & Bromley, Max. Crime and justice in America: a human perspective. West. '95.

Thomas, Andrew Peyton. Crime and the sacking of America: the roots of chaos. Brassey's: UK. '94.

Tonry, Michael. Malign neglect: race, crime, and punishment in America. Oxford University Press. '95.

Trager, Oliver, ed. Crime in America: the war at home. Facts on File. '88.

Tunnell, Kenneth D., ed. Political crime in contemporary America. Garland. '93.

Weisheit, Ralph A., Falcone, David N. & Wells, Edward L. Crime and policing in rural and small-town America. Waveland. '96.

Williams, Christopher. Invisible victims: crime and abuse against people with learning disabilities. J. Kingsley. '95.

Williams, Willie L. & Henderson, Bruce B. Taking back our streets: fighting crime in America. Scribner. '96.

ADDITIONAL PERIODICAL ARTICLES WITH ABSTRACTS

For those who wish to read more widely on the subject of crime in America, this section contains abstracts of additional articles that bear on the topic. Readers who require a comprehensive list of materials are advised to consult the *Readers' Guide Abstracts* and other Wilson publications.

Life in the 90's. Terry Golway. *America* 174:6 F 24 '96

America remains a very violent place despite falling crime rates. Although most major cities in the United States are witnessing annual, double-digit decreases in major crimes, there is no reason to celebrate considering the level of crime that remains. Murders in New York, for example, dropped from 2,245 in 1990 to 1,182 in 1995, which is still a terrible body count for a nation at peace.

The national prospect. Joseph Epstein. *Commentary* 100:49–51 N '95

Part of an issue on America's prospects as a nation. The poor state of American universities and public schools, the breakdown of families, and crime, especially that committed by the young, are the contributing factors to the gloomy prospects for America. The linchpin required to put things back together is the family, and we need to develop ways to strengthen them. Although it is still too early to judge if the Republicans are going to be able to strengthen families, but it is hoped that the Democrats have learned that most Americans are not impressed by their demonstrations of false virtue combined with policies that have led to genuine misery. Unfortunately, whether liberal or conservative, left-wing or right-wing, politicians remain politicians and only an idiot would place full confidence in any of them.

The way we really were. Aaron W. Godfrey. *Commonweal* 122:62 F 24 '95

In the last two decades, the middle-class Irish who have made it in American society have become increasingly worried about drugs and crime among the poor and people of color, yet they fail to see the parallel to their own struggle with alcohol during the Depression. Drug use today is often caused by the same poverty, frustration, and failure that Irish families experienced in America during that earlier era. Like alcohol, drugs help the victim forget, but they also destroy families and relationships. The difference is that alcohol is socially acceptable and portrayed by the media as sophisticated, while the demons that it created have been forgotten amid nostalgia for the "good old days."

Cracking the Net. Joe Chidley. *Maclean's* 108:54–6 My 22 '95

Part of a cover story on crime on the Internet. A new wave of network hacking is posing fresh problems for companies, universities, and law-enforcement officials in industrialized countries. A hacker is defined as an inquisitive, sometimes malicious computer user who, fueled by greed or self-aggrandizement, interrupts data flow and turns it to his own ends. While most hackers are people who simply love playing with computers and who break security measures in a network only for fun or to point out flaws, there is a malicious subset of hackers known as "crackers," who intrude on computer networks to cause damage, commit fraud, or steal data. According to the Computer Emergency Response Team, a nonprofit group that monitors security iosues throughout North America, there were 132 computer intrusions in 1989; in 1994, reports the organization, there were 2,341 invasions.

Prisons for profit. Carl Mollins. *Maclean's* 108:34–6 Je 5 '95

The American public is demanding sterner action against crime and harsher punishment for criminals, and the government has responded with a host of anti-crime measures. The latest trends in penal treatment are hard time and privatized prisons. Alabama's Limestone Correctional Facility has revived the use of chain gangs to cut grass along the highway in an effort at crime deterrence by retribution. Nashville, Tenn.'s Metro-Davidson County Detention Facility, run by Corrections Corp. of America (CCA), aims to encourage inmates to quit crime, and thus reduce the prison population, by rehabilitation. Both reflect an attempt to deal with the growing costs of incarceration. The article discusses the financial success of CCA and other private prison operators and proposed anti-crime laws likely to increase the U.S. prison population.

Top cops. Morgan O. Reynolds. *National Review* 47:56+ F 20 '95

The *Contract With America*'s crime initiative, the "Taking Back Our Streets Act," is based on the faulty premise that crime is a national problem that requires a national solution. The Contract's bill cobbles together old GOP proposals intended to marginally improve bad legislation from the old Democratic Congress. Nearly every provision of "Taking Back Our Streets" suggests the frightening prospect of a gradual nationalization of police, courts, and corrections. A truly new Republican bill would terminate federal activism and devolve power to the states, in accordance with the Tenth Amendment. A good start for the new GOP Congress would be to repeal the entire Clinton Crime Control Act of 1994 and the Brady Gun Control Law.

Scary kids around the corner. Mortimer B. Zuckerman. *U.S. News & World Report* 119:96 D 4 '95

Violent crime is down marginally, but demographic trends suggest that there will be at least 500,000 more males in the dangerous age group in the next five years. Typically, some 6 percent of these turn out to be violent criminals, many as a result of alienation caused by the destruction of the family. The sense that no safe havens exist and that the police cannot protect the nation from violent strangers has led to the employment of 1.5 million private police to provide the protection not furnished by the public police. America should view the investment in new police officers as a deposit in the long and expensive war to make the nation safe again.

Stop! Cyberthief! Michael R. Meyer. *Newsweek* 125:36–8 F 6 '95

Computer crime is probably the fastest-growing brand of wrongdoing in America. Lonely, sick people are stalking women and children on computer networks. Digital thieves are defrauding widows, running securities scams, purloining credit cards, and hacking government and industrial secrets. In a study of 1,271 companies conducted by the leading consulting firm Ernst & Young, half of them reported financial losses from security breaches and digital thievery over the last two years. Unlike real-world theft, however, few electronic crimes are reported, and many are never detected. Given that securities regulators are mostly powerless to stop such things, PC users must protect themselves from becoming victims.

Body bags at 11. Max Frankel. *The New York Times Magazine* 24Ap 2 '95

Local television news is obsessed with crime and disaster, encouraging fear or smug comfort, or both. "A Day in the Life of Local TV News in America," a pamphlet assessing the content of one night's local news on 50 stations in 29 cities, found that the average commercial station devoted less than 13 minutes out of 30 to general news and that the news segments were dominated by stories involving either crime or disaster. Sports and weather averaged a little more than 6 minutes, and commercials claimed nearly 8½ minutes. "Fluff"—trivial features, anchor chatter, celebrity items, and teasers about the news to come after commercials—stood, on average, at a 1 to 3 ratio with general news. The customary excuse for the low quality of local news is that viewers won't stay around for anything better, but few stations employ enough talent to test that proposition.

Experts on crime warn of a ticking time bomb. Fox Butterfield. *New York Times* 6 Ja 6 '96

The Council on Crime in America, an organization of prosecutors and law-enforcement experts, issued a report yesterday calling violent crime in the United States a "ticking time bomb." The report says that crime will explode in the next few years as the number of teenagers soars. The organization painted a bleak portrait of the criminal justice system, maintaining that it remained "a revolving door" that allowed large numbers of violent felons to go free and commit more crimes.

New frontier for gangs: Indian reservations. Seth Mydans. *New York Times* 1+ Mr 18 '95

March 11, 1995—The urban problem of gang warfare has begun to spread to dozens of scattered Indian reservations in the West. Some young Navajos, Apaches, Sioux, and others have imported a gang culture that is alien to their elders.

Crime: safer streets, yet greater fear. Elaine Shannon. *Time* 145:63+ Ja 30

Part of a special section on the state of America. People are more afraid of crime than ever, even though the crime rate has actually fallen over the last 2½ years. Crime is now a bigger concern to Americans than joblessness or the federal deficit; in a recent *Time/CNN* poll, 89 percent of those surveyed said that they believe that crime is getting worse. Yet according to data collected by the FBI, the rate of all crimes dropped 4 percent from 1991 to 1992 and 3.1 percent from 1992 to 1993. Violence-ridden cities from New York to Los Angeles have enjoyed a drop in crime in general and in murder rates in particular. Experts see no dissonance between the somber national mood and the upbeat figures, however. The effect of three decades of rising crime has been cumulative, and it is a rare family that has been unaffected. In addition, crime is no longer geographically or demographically contained, the nature of crime has changed, and more of the perpetrators are juveniles.

Washington's misdirected efforts in curbing crime. William Niskanen. *USA Today* 124:22–4 Jl '95

The Violent Crime Control Law Enforcement Act of 1994 is an outrage. Some of the provision's acts are inconsistent with the Constitution and the historical limits on the powers of Federal government. Others are an abuse of civil liberties or are counterproductive. Moreover, the act's banning of 19 types of semiautomatic rifles is purely symbolic. The article describes the two measures used by the Department of Justice to gauge the level and composition of crime in the U.S. and discusses how these measures tell different stories about crime in America.

The economics of crime. Edwin Rubenstein. *Vital Speeches of the Day* 62:19–21 O 15 '95

An economics analyst from the National Review delivers a speech [February 9, 1995] to the Center for Constructive Alternatives at Hillsdale College in Hillsdale, MI. He looks at the increasing rate of crime in America and blames much of it on the decline of intact families. He then states that the government needs to invent harsher penalties for crime, since the current ones do not deter would-be criminals.

Turning the corner on crime. Steve Sax. *Vital Speeches of the Day* 61:402–3 Ap 15 '95

In an address delivered at the Annual Awards Banquet of the Sacramento County Sheriff's Department in California on February 21, 1995, a professional baseball player discusses crime in America. He asserts that although prevention and education are important tools in fighting crime, deterrence is the real key.